Scandinavian Unexceptionalism

SCANDINAVIAN UNEXCEPTIONALISM

Culture, Markets and the Failure of
Third-Way Socialism

NIMA SANANDAJI

Institute of
Economic Affairs

First published in Great Britain in 2015 by
The Institute of Economic Affairs
2 Lord North Street
Westminster
London SW1P 3LB
in association with London Publishing Partnership Ltd
www.londonpublishingpartnership.co.uk

The mission of the Institute of Economic Affairs is to improve understanding
of the fundamental institutions of a free society by analysing and expounding
the role of markets in solving economic and social problems.

ISBN 978-0-255-36704-2

Many IEA publications are translated into languages other
than English or are reprinted. Permission to translate or to reprint
should be sought from the Director General at the address above.

Typeset in Kepler by T&T Productions Ltd
www.tandtproductions.com

Printed and bound in Great Britain by Page Bros

CONTENTS

THE AUTHOR

Nima Sanandaji is a Swedish author of Kurdish origin who holds a PhD from the Royal Institute of Technology in Stockholm. He has published 15 books on policy issues such as women's career opportunities, integration, entrepreneurship and reforms which encourage innovation in the provision of public services. Nima is a research fellow at the Centre for Policy Studies in London.

FOREWORD

I am regularly amazed at the persistence of several tenacious fallacies regarding the Nordic countries. In this tightly argued monograph Nima Sanandaji has performed a service by addressing them one by one and marshalling evidence and logic to explain the history of Nordic economic success and the genesis, impact and reform of their welfare states. No one who reads this work will be able to repeat, at least not without a bad conscience, the familiar slogans about Nordic socialism, third-way policies or how high taxes and state-guaranteed incomes beget economic growth and engender and nurture moral responsibility and community spirit.

The lag between perception and reality is especially glaring in the case of the Swedish model. Outside Sweden the serious reforms initiated in the 1990s seem not to have been noticed and 'third wayers' continue to act as if Sweden had not liberalised the economy, introduced competition in the production of government-funded services, lowered tax rates and reformed state benefit systems. To most of the 'Swedish model' boosters, it is still 1975.

It is an easily overlooked truism that a redistributive system presupposes something to redistribute. The Nordic countries enjoyed robustly productive economic systems before the welfare states we know today were established. Starting in the 19th century, the peoples of the Nordic countries created vast amounts of wealth, founded new firms and industries, and generated societies with high degrees of social trust and moral responsibility. They built on foundations that, as a result of their histories (notably the relative absence of feudalism) were comparatively egalitarian and mono-ethnic. That wealth and those social orders preceded the welfare state; indeed, without them, the Nordic experiments in welfare statism would have certainly turned out quite differently, as experiences in other countries suggest. After welfare states were initiated, however, the Nordic countries began to coast on accumulated capital. Even more worrying, the strong social trust that was so widespread among the people and that limited predatory behaviour, shirking and disregard for the interests of one's neighbours has been undermined by tax rates that punish those who contribute and transfer payments that encourage those who take. The rising percentage of the populations on disability and early retirement, in an age of improving health and longevity, suggests a population in which shirking has become more and more socially acceptable. The long-term prognosis for such a model is not a happy one.

The comparison of Nordic populations with their cousins who decamped for the US, which forms a small but interesting part of Sanandaji's analysis, suggests that when pundits praise, say, Swedish healthcare by looking at longevity, what they are measuring is not the impact of the Swedish health financing system, but of Swedishness, whether in diet, genetic inheritance or behaviour. Indeed, Americans of Nordic descent exceed their stay-at-home cousins in high degrees of social trust, high incomes and low levels of poverty. It turns out that 'culture matters' and 'culture' is not merely a placeholder for 'all the stuff we cannot understand' but can be measured and studied in terms of behaviour. Cultural capital, and not only physical capital, matters and, like physical capital, cultural capital does not automatically renew itself: it can be eroded over time by perverse incentives.

There is one small matter that Sanandaji does not explore in depth, but it deserves a mention. He quotes Jeffrey Sachs opining that 'In strong and vibrant democracies, a generous social-welfare state is not a road to serfdom but rather to fairness, economic equality and international competitiveness'. Sachs thus suggested that F. A. Hayek in his book *The Road to Serfdom* argued that the welfare state would lead to serfdom. The book argued something rather different: that the nationalisation of the means of production and imposition of centralised planning would undermine liberalism and democracy. The mistake is very common among those who prefer not to read authors to whom they allude, but it is especially common in discussion of the topic that Nima Sanandaji has explored so well.

Sanandaji's monograph should be of interest to anyone who wants to understand the welfare state and the success of the Nordic countries. More broadly, it provides a stimulating occasion for speculation on the future of welfare states everywhere.

Tom G. Palmer

Executive Vice President for International Programs, Atlas Network,
Senior Fellow, Cato Institute,
Editor, After the Welfare State

The views expressed in this monograph are, as in all IEA publications, those of the author and not those of the Institute (which has no corporate view), its managing trustees, Academic Advisory Council members or senior staff. With some exceptions, such as with the publication of lectures, all IEA monographs are blind peer-reviewed by at least two academics or researchers who are experts in the field.

SUMMARY

- Left-leaning pop stars, politicians, journalists, political commentators and academics have long praised Scandinavian countries for their high levels of welfare provision and for their economic and social outcomes. It is, indeed, true that they are successful by most reasonable measures.
- However, Scandinavia's success story predated the welfare state. Furthermore, Sweden began to fall behind as the state grew rapidly from the 1960s. Between 1870 and 1936, Sweden enjoyed the highest growth rate in the industrialised world. However, between 1936 and 2008, the growth rate was only 13th out of 28 industrialised nations. Between 1975 and the mid-1990s, Sweden dropped from being the 4th richest nation in the world to the 13th richest nation in the world.
- As late as 1960, tax revenues in the Nordic nations ranged between 25 per cent of GDP in Denmark to 32 per cent in Norway – similar to other developed countries. At the current time, Scandinavian countries are again no longer outliers when it comes to levels of government spending and taxation.
- The third-way radical social democratic era in Scandinavia, much admired by the left, only lasted

from the early 1970s to the early 1990s. The rate of
business formation during the third-way era was
dreadful. In 2004, 38 of the 100 businesses with the
highest revenues in Sweden had started as privately
owned businesses within the country. Of these firms,
just two had been formed after 1970. None of the 100
largest firms ranked by employment were founded
within Sweden after 1970. Furthermore, between 1950
and 2000, although the Swedish population grew from
7 million to almost 9 million, net job creation in the
private sector was close to zero.

- Scandinavia is often cited as having high life
  expectancy and good health outcomes in areas such as
  infant mortality. Again, this predates the expansion of
  the welfare state. In 1960, Norway had the highest life
  expectancy in the OECD, followed by Sweden, Iceland
  and Denmark in third, fourth and fifth positions. By
  2005, the gap in life expectancy between Scandinavian
  countries and both the UK and the US had shrunk
  considerably. Iceland, with a moderately sized
  welfare sector, has over time outpaced the four major
  Scandinavian countries in terms of life expectancy
  and infant mortality.

- Scandinavia's more equal societies also developed well
  before the welfare states expanded. Income inequality
  reduced dramatically during the last three decades of
  the 19th century and during the first half of the 20th
  century. Indeed, most of the shift towards greater
  equality happened before the introduction of a large
  public sector and high taxes.

- The development of Scandinavian welfare states has led to a deterioration in social capital. Despite the fact that Nordic nations are characterised by good health, only the Netherlands spends more on incapacity-related unemployment than Scandinavian countries. A survey from 2001 showed that 44 per cent believed that it was acceptable to claim sickness benefits if they were dissatisfied with their working environment. Other studies have pointed to increases in sickness absence due to sporting events. For instance, absence among men due to sickness increased by 41 per cent during the 2002 football World Cup. These shifts in working norms have also been tracked in the World Value Survey. In the 1981–84 survey, 82 per cent of Swedes agreed with the statement 'claiming government benefits to which you are not entitled is never justifiable'; in the 2010–14 survey, only 55 per cent of Swedes believed that it was never right to claim benefits to which they were not entitled.

- Another regrettable feature of Scandinavian countries is their difficulty in assimilating immigrants. Unemployment rates of immigrants with low education levels in Anglo-Saxon countries are generally equal to or lower than unemployment rates among natives with a similar educational background, whereas in Scandinavian countries they are much higher. In Scandinavian labour markets, even immigrants with high qualifications can struggle to find suitable employment. Highly educated immigrants in Finland and Sweden have an unemployment rate over

8 percentage points higher than native-born Finns and Swedes of a similar educational background. This compares with very similar employment rates between the two groups in Anglo-Saxon countries.

- The descendants of Scandinavian migrants in the US combine the high living standards of the US with the high levels of equality of Scandinavian countries. Median incomes of Scandinavian descendants are 20 per cent higher than average US incomes. It is true that poverty rates in Scandinavian countries are lower than in the US. However, the poverty rate among descendants of Nordic immigrants in the US today is half the average poverty rate of Americans – this has been a consistent finding for decades. In fact, Scandinavian Americans have lower poverty rates than Scandinavian citizens who have not emigrated. This suggests that pre-existing cultural norms are responsible for the low levels of poverty among Scandinavians rather than Nordic welfare states.
- Many analyses of Scandinavian countries conflate correlation with causality. It is very clear that many of the desirable features of Scandinavian societies, such as low income inequality, low levels of poverty and high levels of economic growth, predated the development of the welfare state. It is equally clear that high levels of trust also predated the era of high government spending and taxation. All these indicators began to deteriorate after the expansion of the Scandinavian welfare states and the increase in taxes necessary to fund it.

EDITORIAL NOTE

The IEA monograph and book series have been reorganised to better reflect the nature of the different types of publications we produce. There are now two series, Hobart Paperbacks and Readings in Political Economy. The former series includes more directly policy-oriented publications and longer studies of a particular area of economics. Effectively, this series will be a merger of the former Hobart Papers, Hobart Paperbacks and Research Monographs. The first Hobart Paperback in the new format therefore took the number following that of the last Hobart Paper. Readings in Political Economy will include primers, lectures and more philosophical works. This publication is the first in that new series.

TABLES AND FIGURES

1 UNDERSTANDING NORDIC SUCCESS

It is a country whose very name has become a synonym for a materialist paradise. [...] No slums disfigure their cities, their air and water are largely pollution free... Neither ill health, unemployment nor old age pose the terror of financial hardship.

Time Magazine (1976), describing Sweden as a social democratic utopia

The left's admiration for the Nordics

During a visit to Paris, Bruce Springsteen explained that his dream was for the US to adopt a Swedish style welfare state (Nyheter 2012; Business Insider 2012). The famous musician is far from alone in idealising Scandinavian policies. The four Nordic nations (Denmark, Finland, Norway and Sweden) are often regarded as prime role models, the policies of which should be emulated by others. Internationally, advocates of left-of-centre policies view these countries as examples of how high-tax social democratic systems are viable and successful. Paul Krugman, for example, has said: 'Every time I read someone talking about the "collapsing welfare states of Europe", I have this urge to take that person on a forced walking tour of Stockholm' (*New York Times* 2011).

The admiration of Nordic welfare state policies is far from a new phenomenon. The political scientist John Logue argued in 1979: 'A simple visual comparison of Scandinavian towns with American equivalents provides strong evidence that reasonably efficient welfare measures can abolish poverty as it was known in the past; economic growth alone, as the American case indicates, does not' (Logue 1979: 75). Logue believed that the greatest threat to the Nordic welfare states was that they were too successful; eliminating social problems to such a degree that people forgot the importance of welfare policies (Logue 1979, 1985).

In 1994 David Popenoe wrote that 'Scandinavian welfare and family policies are the envy of [left] liberal-thinking people around the world'. The author continued to remark that he, 'like most American social researchers', was 'largely in support of the Scandinavians' accomplishments in the area of social welfare'.[1] In 2006 Jeffrey Sachs argued in *Scientific American* that the ideas of liberal economist F. A. Hayek were proven wrong by the Nordic social democracies: 'In strong and vibrant democracies, a generous social-welfare state is not a road to serfdom but rather to fairness, economic equality and international competitiveness' (Sachs 2006: 42). This list of admirers could be easily extended.

---

1 In the article the author did mention that there were indeed also drawbacks to the generous welfare systems supported by high taxes (Popenoe 1994: 78).

The high regard comes as no surprise. Nordic societies are uniquely successful. Not only are they characterised by high living standards, but also by other attractive features such as low crime rates, long life expectancies, high degrees of social cohesion and even income distributions. Various international rankings conclude that they are among the best, if not the best, places in the world in which to live. One example is the 'Better Life Index', complied by the Organisation for Economic Cooperation and Development (OECD). In the 2014 edition of the index Norway was ranked as the nation with the second highest level of well-being in the world, followed by Sweden and Denmark in third and fourth position. Finland ranked as the eighth best country (Table 1).

Table 1 Ranking in the 2014 edition of the OECD 'Better Life Index'

1.	Australia
2.	Norway
3.	Sweden
4.	Denmark
5.	Canada
6.	Switzerland
7.	United States
8.	Finland
9.	The Netherlands
10.	New Zealand

Source: The Huffington Post (2014).

Another example is the 2013 edition of Mothers' Index Rankings, where Save the Children rates nations depending on how favourable their social and economic systems are for the well-being of mothers and children. Finland ranks as the best country in the world in this regard, followed by Norway and Sweden in second and third place respectively. Denmark is in sixth position (Save the Children 2014).[2]

---

2 In the previous year's index, the four Nordic countries had the same positions with the exception that Sweden was ranked second and Norway third (Save the Children 2013).

If one disregards the importance of thinking carefully about causality, the argument for adopting a Scandinavian-style economic policy in other nations seems obvious. The Nordic nations – in particular Sweden, which is most often used as an international role model – have large welfare states and are successful. This is often seen as proof that a third-way policy between socialism and capitalism works well, and that other societies can reach the same favourable social outcomes simply by expanding the size of government. If one studies Nordic history and society in depth, however, it quickly becomes evident that the simplistic analysis is flawed.

Is it only welfare states that make Nordic countries different?

The experience in Sweden, Denmark, Finland and Norway could also easily be used to argue for the benefits of policies oriented towards free markets. It can also be used as a warning of the economic and social problems that can arise when government involvement in society becomes too large. To understand the Nordic experience one must bear in mind that the large welfare state is not the only thing that sets these countries apart from the rest of the world.[3]

---

3   The other Nordic nations, namely the Faroe Islands, Åland Islands, Greenland and Iceland, are not the focus of this book. The reason is that they have small populations and very different geographical circumstances from the rest of the world. With the exception of Iceland, they are autonomous parts of the four major Nordic countries rather than independent states.

The countries also have homogeneous populations with non-governmental social institutions that are uniquely adapted to the modern world. High levels of trust, a strong work ethic, civic participation, social cohesion, individual responsibility and family values are long-standing features of Nordic society that predate the welfare state. These deeper social institutions explain why Sweden, Denmark and Norway could so quickly grow from impoverished nations to wealthy ones as industrialisation and the market economy were introduced in the late 19th century. They also played an important role in Finland's growing prosperity after World War II.

The same norms explain why large welfare systems could be implemented in the mid-20th century. A strong work ethic and high levels of trust made it possible to levy high taxes and offer generous benefits with limited risk of abuse and undesirable incentive effects. It is important to stress that the direction of causality seems to be from cultures with strong social capital towards welfare states that have not had serious adverse consequences, and not the other way around. Also, cultural traits adapt slowly. It took time to build up the exceptionally high levels of social capital in Nordic cultures. And it took time for generous welfare models to begin undermining the countries' strong work ethic.

Culture and welfare states

Why do Nordic societies have unusually strong emphasis on individual responsibility and strong social capital?

Religion, climate and history all seem to have played a role in forming these unique cultures. Over a hundred years ago, German sociologist Max Weber observed that Protestant countries in northern Europe tended to have a higher living standard, more high-quality academic institutions and overall stronger social cohesion than Catholic and Orthodox countries. Weber believed that the cause of the success of Protestant nations was to be found in a stronger 'Protestant work ethic' (see, for example, Nelson 2010).

According to Swedish scholar Assar Lindbeck, it has historically been difficult to survive as an agriculturalist without working exceptionally hard in the hostile Scandinavian environment. The population therefore out of necessity adopted a culture with a great emphasis on individual responsibility and hard work (see, for example, Lindbeck 1995, 2003). What is unique about Nordic nations is not only that they are cold, but also that throughout most of their recent history they have been dominated by independent farmers.

Most other parts of Europe had feudal systems, where much of the population were serfs who lacked private ownership of their land. With the exception of Denmark, feudalism did not manage to get the same grip in the Nordics. Many farmers have historically owned their own land in Scandinavia. Hard work has historically not only been a necessity in the cold north, but also been clearly rewarding due to the presence of widespread private ownership.

The homogeneous Nordic countries have adopted cultures with strong social cohesion, resulting in the highest levels of trust in the world (Delhy and Newton 2005; Berggren et al. 2008). This is maintained when Scandinavians move abroad: among the US population those with Scandinavian origins have the highest levels of trust. Americans of Scandinavian descent even have slightly higher levels of trust than the populations of Scandinavian countries themselves (Uslander 2008; Sanandaji 2010a). This suggests that the origin of the Nordic culture of success predates modern welfare states. After all, large-scale migration of Scandinavians to the US occurred during the late 19th century and the early 20th century, before the shift towards welfare state policies.

High levels of trust, a strong work ethic and social cohesion are the perfect starting point for successful economies. They are also cornerstones of fruitful social democratic welfare policies – a pre-existing high level of social cohesion allows welfare states and high taxes to be implemented without the same impact on work habits as such policies might have in a different environment. As argued below, however, welfare policies can affect culture in the long term. Even the well-functioning societies in Nordic nations have with time been adversely impacted by welfare dependency and the impact of high taxation on incentives. The Nordic countries have not only introduced welfare states, but also experimented with socialism in the form of a planned economy. This is at least true of Sweden, which through its famous third-way policies attempted to achieve a form of 'market socialism'. Third-way policies were, however, reversed and can be viewed as a short-lived and failed experiment.

The ebb and flow of free-market policies in Sweden

Throughout most of its modern history Sweden has had a favourable business environment. The period character-ised by the most extensive welfare state policies (around 1970–95), when the country clearly deviated from market policies, is an exception. As it happens, this period was associated with stagnant economic development, in terms of GDP growth as well as job creation and entrepreneur-ship. The history of the other Nordic nations parallels that of Sweden in this regard.

It is true that Nordic nations maintain a high standard of living, despite steep taxes. But it is wrong to see this as proof that high taxes do not affect the economy. Except for the short and unsuccessful period mentioned above, Nordic nations have tended to combine high taxes with an environ-ment of business freedom and free trade. Indeed, studies show that high taxes significantly hinder economic develop-ment in Scandinavian countries. While affluent, the Nordic nations could have been even more affluent with lower tax rates. It is true that the welfare services that are supported by high taxes provide various benefits. At the same time, many of the favourable social outcomes in these societies were evident before the creation of extensive welfare states.

Indeed, generous welfare policies have created new social problems, though with a substantial time lag as might be expected. The combination of high taxes, gen-erous government benefits and a rigid labour market has led to dependency on government handouts among large subsections of the population. Families have thus become trapped in poverty. The policies have, in particular, limited the ability of the societies to integrate immigrants into their labour markets.

Today the Nordic economies are again growing, following a return to broadly free-market policies that served them well before policies changed during the 1960s and 1970s. The countries are changing in the face of serious long-term problems that have developed over the last 30 years. Oil-rich Norway has implemented modest changes, and is also facing serious challenges, including a deteriorating work ethic among its youth. Finland, Sweden and Denmark have on the other hand introduced far-reaching market reforms. These changes include greater openness to trade, clear reductions in the tax burden, private provision of welfare services, the introduction of personal retirement accounts and, in Denmark, even a shift towards a liberal labour market.

A key lesson from the success of Nordic society is that what can broadly be defined as 'culture' matters. We should not be surprised that it is these nations, with their historically strong work ethic and community-based social institutions, that have had fewer adverse effects from welfare states and are therefore used as the poster child for those wishing to extol the benefits of active welfare policies. On the other hand, southern European countries with similar sized welfare states and size of government have had less favourable outcomes.[4]

---

4   This is further explored in Sanandaji (2012a).

Lastly, it should be emphasised that descendants of Scandinavians who migrated to the US in the 19th century are still characterised by favourable social outcomes, such as a low poverty rate and high employment. This is an important point that the left in countries such as the UK and the US should note. There are similar outcomes for Scandinavian people in different policy environments: in other words, there is nothing exceptional about Scandinavians living in Scandinavia. Furthermore, the normal economic laws prevail: a good cultural background leads to good economic outcomes; and high taxes and a large welfare state ultimately undermine both the culture and the economy. In this respect, Scandinavia is entirely unexceptional. Deeper social factors such as culture and non-governmental social institutions have played, and continue to play, an important role in Nordic success.

This book explores the ideas stated above in greater detail. The starting point is how Nordic culture paved the way for phenomenal wealth creation. This occurred when industrialisation and free-market systems were introduced into previously poor agrarian societies.

2 THE SCANDINAVIAN FREE-MARKET SUCCESS STORY

In the period from 1870 to 1970 the Nordic countries were among the world's fastest-growing countries, thanks to a series of pro-business reforms such as the establishment of banks and the privatisation of forests. But in the 1970s and 1980s the undisciplined growth of government caused the reforms to run into the sands.

The Economist (2013a)

A few years ago, US National Public Radio ran a story 'about a country that seems to violate the laws of the economic universe.' The country had 'one of the lowest poverty rates in the world, low unemployment, a steadily growing economy and almost no corruption' although it had high taxes. That country was Denmark (National Public Radio 2010).

A popular notion is that the Scandinavian countries manage to defy standard economic logic, by prospering despite large welfare systems and state involvement in the economy. Sweden's former social democratic Prime Minister Göran Persson has compared the country's economy to a bumblebee: 'With its overly heavy body and little wings, supposedly it should not be able to fly – but it does' (quoted by

Thakur et al. 2003: iii). In reality, however, the economic development that has occurred in Nordic nations is anything but mysterious. The nation's prosperity developed during periods characterised by free-market policies, low or moderate taxes and limited state involvement in the economy.

Early Scandinavian success

The Scandinavian free-market success story is well worth telling. And, in fact, it was told already in a 1943 research paper by James Beddy. The Irish historian asked a simple question: how come Denmark had grown so much more prosperous than Ireland? Based on a thorough statistical analysis Beddy concluded that Denmark had a national income per head that was almost 50 per cent higher than in Ireland. But natural factors such as average temperature, hours of sunshine, rainfall and abundance of natural resources all favoured Ireland (Beddy 1943).

Seven decades ago the success of Denmark was already something of a puzzle. And the answer was not the welfare state, since that institution was just developing. Social democratic policies could hardly explain why Denmark had grown so rich in the late 19th century and at the beginning of the 20th century. Beddy wrote (ibid.: 189):

> Denmark is not only a smaller country than Eire but her climate is less equable, her soils are, in general, lighter and poorer, she has no coal and no water power to compensate for its absence, nor has she any iron ore or other metallic ores to serve as a basis for industrial activities.

Yet, in comparison with Eire, she has a bigger population, a greater agricultural output, a more extensive industrial system, a larger foreign trade, a lower national debt, a higher national income and a better standard of living.

According to the Irish economist, the main reason for Denmark's success was that its economic system differed from that of Ireland. Ireland could learn from Denmark by focusing on 'stimulating maximum profitable agricultural activity' and taking greater advantage of international trade. A key element was that the new 'system shall be free from the restrictive effects of [Ireland's] present one' (ibid.: 208). In other words, Denmark was richer than Ireland despite a less favorable climate and fewer natural resources, since it relied more on market forces.

More than a half century later, Kevin O'Rourke expanded on this analysis. The Irish professor of economic history explored the structural and social differences that had existed between Ireland and Denmark in the late 19th century. According to O'Rourke the latter country's greater prosperity has several explanations. Denmark had a homogeneous culture coupled with political stability: Ireland was, on the other hand, culturally and politically divided. Danish society in addition benefited from higher levels of trust and social capital. This can explain why cooperative businesses such as creameries could more easily be founded and run by milk farmers in Denmark than in Ireland (O'Rourke 2006).

The countries also had different backgrounds when it came to how policy was developed. Denmark was an independent nation, the 'generally liberal policies' of which had resulted from Danish decisions. Irish liberalism was a product of British decisions. Reforms transferring land ownership from landlords to farmers had occurred much earlier in Denmark than in Ireland. O'Rourke explained that Irish farmers had limited access to capital they needed to grow. On the other hand, small local savings banks in Denmark supplied credit even to those with little or no security for loans (ibid.).

In another publication, O'Rourke explains how the lack of market forces resulted in Ireland being slower in adapting novel technologies for dairy production than Denmark – an important business at the time for both nations (O'Rourke 2003: 1):

> Separators and cooperatives spread much more quickly in Denmark than in Ireland, despite the fact that both countries were important dairy producers, located in north-west Europe, and selling to the same market (Britain) [...] [P]roperty rights and social capital played a crucial role in determining the extent to which these two innovations were adopted: a lack of social and political cohesion, uncertain property rights as well as cultural factors all help explain why Ireland lagged behind Denmark during this period.

The comparison between Ireland and Denmark clearly illustrates the benefits of combining the unique Nordic culture with free-market capitalism. Already during the latter half of the 19th century Denmark thrived through a combination of large-scale and small-scale entrepreneurship. Large successful firms competed with cooperative movements and small artisan firms (Kristensen 1989).

Denmark's closest neighbour to the north was more of a late-bloomer. However, few other nations have demonstrated as clearly as Sweden the phenomenal economic growth that comes from adopting free-market policies. Sweden was a poor nation before the 1870s, resulting in massive emigration to the US. As a capitalist system evolved out of the agrarian society, the country grew richer. Property rights, free markets and the rule of law combined with large numbers of well-educated engineers and entrepreneurs. These factors created an environment in which Sweden enjoyed an unprecedented period of sustained and rapid economic development.

In the hundred years following the market liberalisation of the late 19th century and the onset of industrialisation, Sweden experienced phenomenal economic growth (Maddison 1982). Famous Swedish companies such as IKEA, Volvo, Tetra Pak, H&M, Ericsson and Alfa Laval were all founded during this period, and were aided by business-friendly economic policies and low taxes (Sanandaji 2010b).

It is sometimes claimed that Sweden's high growth rate is a result of social democratic policies. In fact, much of the development occurred between the time when free markets developed (circa 1870) and the start of the era dominated by social democratic rule (circa 1936). Economic historian Angus Maddison's database of estimated historic per capita GDP makes it possible to calculate growth rates for 28 OECD countries (Maddison 2010).

Figure 1 GDP per capita growth 1870–1970

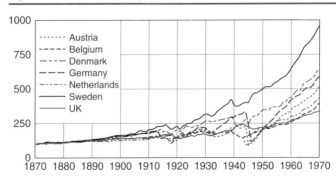

Source: Maddison (2010) and own calculations. GDP per capita is shown for each country compared with the level in 1870 normalised to 100.

Between 1870 and 1936, Sweden enjoyed the highest growth rate in the industrialised world. However, between 1936 and 2008, the growth rate was only 13th out of 28 industrialised nations.[1] It is important to realise that Sweden remained a relatively free-market-oriented nation for several decades after the beginning of the social democratic era. The policy shift occurred slowly over time. It was at the beginning of the 1970s when the fiscal burden and government spending in Sweden reached high levels relative to other industrialised countries.

---

[1] This result is not sensitive to the exact years chosen for the start of the social democratic era. If we instead define the start of the era as 1932, the results are broadly similar. Sweden had the highest growth among the industrialised countries between 1870 and 1932, and the 15th highest growth during the period 1932–2008.

Figure 1 shows the economic development between 1870 and 1970 in Sweden and other comparable western European countries. During this 100-year period, Sweden was characterised by small-government policies. The country was also neutral in both world wars, avoiding much of the destruction that occurred elsewhere in Europe. This, alongside a catch-up effect, can explain why living standards in Sweden rose three times as rapidly as in the UK. In 1870 Sweden's GDP per capita was 57 per cent lower than in the UK. In 1970 it had risen to become 21 per cent higher.

However, Sweden's wealth creation slowed down following the transition to a high tax burden and a large public sector. Figure 2 shows the development in the same countries from 1970 until the financial crisis of 2008, the end-point of Maddison's Historical Statistics of the World

Figure 2 GDP per capita growth 1970–2008

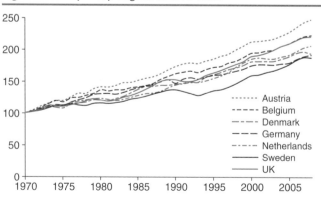

Source: Maddison (2010) and own calculations. GDP per capita is shown for each country compared with the level in 1970 normalised to 100.

Economy. During this period Sweden lagged behind other comparable European countries.

Denmark followed a similar pattern. The social democratic era in Denmark can be said to have begun in 1924. Between 1870 and 1924, Denmark had the 6th highest growth rate in the industrialised world. Between 1924 and 2008, however, Denmark's growth was only ranked 16th compared with other industrialised countries during the same period. As in Sweden, the social democrats in Denmark were initially pragmatic, implementing their policies slowly. The shift from low and moderate taxation to higher levels of taxation occurred around the 1970s. Again, much like Sweden, Denmark experienced strong growth until 1970, but started to lag behind after the transition towards a large public sector (Figures 1 and 2).

Finland followed a different growth trajectory. The nation went from Russian rule to a bloody and failed socialist revolution. Thereafter a welfare state began forming. Finland has historically had lower tax levels than Denmark and Sweden. This also applies to Norway, which has grown rich during later decades thanks to considerable oil wealth.

The slow beginnings of social democracy

All four countries have been characterised by social democratic welfare models. Social democracy has been so entrenched that centre-right parties also played a key part in developing and upholding the welfare systems. However, the progress to social democracy was pragmatic until 1960. As late as 1960, tax revenues in the Nordic nations ranged between 25 per cent of GDP in Denmark to 32 per cent in Norway (Swedish Tax Agency 2007). The four Scandinavian countries at the time had systems of social protection and welfare services supported through moderate tax levels not much different from those of many other developed countries. The policy shift towards bigger governments and higher taxes than other developed countries began during the 1960s and continued in the 1970s.

Table 2   Development of tax take (percentage of GDP)

	1955	1965	1975	1985	1995	2005	2013
Sweden	24	31	39	45	46	47	43
Denmark	23	30	38	45	48	50	49
Finland	27	30	36	39	45	42	44
Norway	28	30	39	43	41	43	41
UK	30	29	34	36	32	34	33
US	24	24	25	25	27	26	25

Source: OECD tax database.

A historical comparison is shown in Table 2. In the UK in the mid 1950s, the proportion of national income taken in tax was higher than in any of the Scandinavian countries. As Nordic policies radicalised in the late 1960s, however, their tax rates soon overtook those of the UK. The early welfare state models, supported by moderate tax levels, were focused on providing services such as education, health care and infrastructure. With time, high taxes and generous welfare systems created a situation where a growing share of the general public became dependent on government welfare payments. Increased reliance on the state can be seen both as an effect of and a cause of the shift from moderate to high levels of taxation in the Scandinavian countries.

Shifting policies

The phenomenal national income growth in the Nordic nations occurred before the rise of large welfare states. The rise in living standards was made possible when cultures based on social cohesion, high levels of trust and strong work ethics were combined with free markets and low taxes. The rise in living standards continued under moderate social democrat policies. Rather than challenging the laws of economics, the Nordic success story reinforces the idea that business-friendly and small-government-oriented policies can promote growth.

The period from around the beginning of the 1960s was characterised by popularisation of radical socialist ideas. In the Nordics, previously pragmatic social democrats radicalised and moved sharply to the left. The turn towards socialism was most strongly felt in Sweden, where the famous so-called third-way orientation was formed. The basic idea was to replace free markets with a model closer to a socialist planned economy. Undermining the basic elements of the market system proved to be a colossal failure in terms of promoting sustainable economic growth. The new model, relying on massive state involvement, was simply not sustainable. The high living standards were a result of the fruits of the previous successful policies. Sweden was no bumblebee that could escape the marring effects of socialist planning.

3   THE FAILURE OF THIRD-WAY POLICIES – ENTREPRENEURSHIP

> If recent developments of the Swedish economic and social system continue, the 'Swedish model' [...] will turn out to have been a brief historical episode – an interlude lasting no more than about three decades, from the mid-1960s to the early 1990s.
>
> Assar Lindbeck (1997: 1314)

A common notion is that particularly Sweden, and to some extent other Nordic nations, have embarked on a unique economic route: the third way. Third-way politics refers to an alternative to free markets on the one hand and communism on the other. Indeed, policies did steer sharply to the left during the late 1960s in Sweden. Not only did the overall tax burden rise, but the new system also discriminated heavily against individuals who owned businesses. As politics radicalised, the social democratic system began challenging the core of the free-market model: entrepreneurship.

The impact of taxes on business owners

Swedish economist Magnus Henrekson has concluded that the effective marginal tax rate (marginal tax plus the

Table 3   Effective marginal taxes per cent (after allowing for
inflation and deductions) in Sweden in 1980

Owner	Debt	New share issues	Retained earnings
Households (private owners)	58	137	52
Tax exempt institutions (such as government pension funds)	–83	–12	11
Insurance companies	–55	38	29

Calculations based on the actual asset composition in manufacturing. A 10 per cent real pre-tax return at actual inflation rates is assumed. The inflation rate for 1980 used in the calculation is 9.4 per cent. Source: Henrekson (2007).

effect of inflation) that was levied on Swedish businesses at times reached more than 100 per cent of their profits. To illustrate this point, Table 3 shows the effective marginal tax rate for different combinations of owners and sources of finance. As can be seen, debt financing consistently received a much more favourable tax treatment compared with equity finance. In addition, the taxation of households was unusually steep due to high general marginal tax rates, high levels of inflation and the combined effect of wealth and income taxation. Family-owned companies in particular were affected by a wealth tax on their net worth. It was not possible to deduct the wealth tax at the company level. Therefore, funds required to pay the wealth tax were first subject to the mandatory payroll tax as well as the personal income tax (Henrekson 2007).[1]

In 1980 a private person who owned a business could pay an effective marginal tax of 137 per cent on the returns on

---

1   The effective marginal tax is calculated assuming a pre-tax real rate of return of 10 per cent.

the capital raised by new share issues. This means that the individual would actually lose money by making a profit once the effect of both taxes and the inflation of the original investment were taken into account. If the business had been financed by debt, the venture became profitable, albeit still facing a high tax rate. Tax-exempt institutions and insurance companies could face negative effective taxation, due mainly to the effect of high rates of inflation (ibid.).

Capitalism without capitalists

Henrekson draws the conclusion that the tax policies were 'developed according to the vision of a market economy without individual capitalists and entrepreneurs' (ibid.: 212). Not surprisingly, the sharp left turn in economic policy markedly affected entrepreneurship. Sten Axelsson, another Swedish economist, has shown that the period between the end of the 19th century and the beginning of World War I was a golden age for the founding of successful entrepreneurial firms in Sweden. After 1970, however, the establishment of new firms dropped significantly (Axelsson 2006).

In 2004, 38 of the 100 businesses with the highest revenues in Sweden were entrepreneurial: in other words started as privately owned businesses within the country. Of these firms, 21 were founded before 1913. Additionally, 15 were founded between 1914 and 1970. Only two had been formed after 1970. If the 100 largest firms are instead ranked according to how many people they employed, none of the largest entrepreneurial firms were founded after 1970 (ibid.).

How can this dramatic fall in entrepreneurship be explained? Why did Sweden become so heavily dependent on firms that were formed generations ago? One reason might be that it takes time for firms to grow large; another, that large firms played a more vital part in the economy in previous times. However, these factors alone cannot explain the massive reduction in the number of new entrepreneurial firms in Sweden. Clearly, one important factor is the changes in economic policy, towards the famous third way between socialism and free markets.

Reliance on a few large companies, often founded more than a century ago, is also common in the other Nordic nations. As an example, Nokia contributed fully a quarter of Finnish growth from 1998 to 2007; this single company, founded in 1865, generated nearly a fifth of the country's exports (*The Economist* 2012).

Social democratic politicians and labour union representatives have long been in favour of an economic system which relies on a few large companies. These employers are seen as stable and it is easy for both the government and the labour unions to negotiate with them. However, systems which favour old economic structures, but which do not encourage entrepreneurship, become less able to adapt. Nokia's recent failures have impacted significantly on Finland's economic well-being. This in turn has spurred a debate about how nascent entrepreneurs can be encouraged.

In Norway, comprehensive state involvement in the economy supported by public oil wealth still today distorts economic dynamism. The Norwegian government owns 37 per cent of the total equity of firms listed on the Oslo stock market. In addition it also controls some non-listed major firms such as Statkraft. If listed, the power-generation firm would be the third largest company on the stock market (*The Economist* 2013b).

The OECD pointed out in 2013 that effective taxes on interest-bearing accounts and shares can reach 113 per cent for private owners in Norway who pay wealth tax, a group including successful entrepreneurs. Private owners who do not pay wealth tax and have invested in owner-occupied housing on the other hand face zero taxation. This situation is, according to the OECD, 'likely to result in significant distortions to saving and investment behaviour' (OECD 2012a: 32).

Unlike Norway, Sweden has in recent years abolished punitive taxes on entrepreneurs. Taxes on profits no longer reach 100 per cent at the margin. Taxes on wealth and inheritance have in fact been abolished. Historically, however, Sweden has been the Nordic nation where third-way policies have been most far-reaching. The hostile attitude towards private owners was in line with the idea of creating capitalism without capitalists.

Employee funds and other forms of socialised ownership

These policies culminated in the introduction of 'employee funds' at the beginning of the 1980s. The idea was to confiscate parts of companies' profits and use them to buy shares, which in turn would be part of the funds controlled by labour unions. In effect, the system was designed to gradually transform the ownership of private companies to the unions – a soft evolution towards socialism. Although the system was abolished before it could turn Sweden into a socialist economy, it did manage to drive the founders of IKEA, Tetra Pak, H&M and other highly successful firms away from the country.

Third-way policies are often upheld as the normal state of Swedish policies. In reality, one can better understand these policies as a social experiment, with poor outcomes in terms of stagnating growth, which has with time been abandoned (see, for example, Lindbeck 1997). Interestingly, even the leading social democrats at the time seem to have been aware of the damage that third-way policies could do.

The most striking example relates to the introduction of the employee funds. Kjell-Olof Feldt, one of Sweden's leading social democrats and at the time the finance minister, had to debate the benefits of the funds in parliament. But the minister was uneasy. During the debate, he was scribbling on a piece of paper. A Swedish reporter took a photograph of a poem that the minister wrote down. Remarkably, it turned out that the finance minister was anything but enthusiastic about the funds. In fact, he believed them to have had a significant negative impact on Sweden. Feldt went as far as describing them using profanity.

Kjell-Olof Feldt had good reasons to be critical of the radical ideas championed and introduced by his own party. In October 1983, a few months before Feldt scribbled his famous poem, what is likely to have been the largest political demonstration in the country's history was arranged.

Upwards of 100,000 people marched against the employee funds. Although the social democratic leadership seems to have been aware that the funds were a bad idea, they had invested too much political prestige in the idea to back away from it.

The funds were introduced in 1984, and later abolished following the election of a centre-right government in 1991. Not only was the confiscation of profits for the funds stopped, the money previously gathered in the funds was transferred into pensions savings and research foundations. Sweden chose to return to the path of market economics over that of socialism.

Poor Scandinavian economic performance

The employee funds were the tip of an iceberg of destructive policies introduced during the third-way period. Changes in regulation, taxation and increased state involvement had reduced the growth potential of the previously dynamic Swedish economy. As late as 1975 Sweden was ranked as the 4th richest nation in the world according to OECD measures. As shown in Table 4, the policy shift that occurred dramatically slowed down the growth rate. Sweden dropped to 13th place in the mid 1990s. In 2010, following a period of recovery from the country's crisis and the free-market reforms that followed, Sweden had risen to 10th position.[2]

---

2   It should be noted that the OECD had 24 member states in 1993, but expanded by the addition of Mexico in 1994, the Czech Republic in 1995, Hungary, South Korea and Poland in 1996, Slovakia in 2000 and Slovenia,

Norway has, thanks to enormous oil wealth, climbed in the rankings. Finland almost dropped out of the top 20 ranking during the mid 1990s, until recovering to 14th position in 2010: this recovery coincided with long-term reforms towards more economic freedom. Denmark's position fell from 7th position to 10th between 1970 and 1980. Three decades later, Denmark had regained its previous ranking, after an impressive array of market-oriented reforms. Of significant sized economies, only Japan, which is a subject of constant discussion for its 'decades of lost growth' and with huge demographic problems, has come anywhere near to dropping so many places as Sweden. It is interesting that the left rarely discusses this calamitous Swedish growth performance from 1970 to 2000, when promoting Swedish-style third-way policies. Even Bo Ringholm, social democratic finance minister in Sweden, has acknowledged this fact. In 2002 he explained: 'If Sweden had had the same growth rates as the OECD average since 1970, our total resources would have been so much greater that it would be the equivalent of 20,000 SEK [$2,700] more per household per month' (Ringholm 2002). It should also be noted that by 2010, by which time Sweden's relative decline had been arrested, government spending in Sweden had fallen to levels not very different from those in other major European economies (including the UK).

Chile, Israel and Estonia in 2010. However, the new arrivals typically have lower purchasing power adjusted GDP per capita levels than the old member states. Thus the enlargement of the OECD member states does not explain Sweden's drop in the wealth league. Sweden had already achieved a low ranking as the 13th richest nation in 1995, before the expansion of the OECD. Source: OECD Stat Extract, own calculations.

Table 4   OECD income league

1970	1980	1990	2000	2010
1. Switzerland	1. Switzerland	1. Luxembourg	1. Luxembourg	1. Luxembourg
2. Luxembourg	2. Luxembourg	2. Switzerland	2. Norway	2. Norway
3. US	3. US	3. US	3. US	3. Switzerland
4. Sweden	4. Iceland	4. Iceland	4. Switzerland	4. US
5. Australia	5. Canada	5. Canada	5. Netherlands	5. Australia
6. Canada	6. Sweden	6. Sweden	6. Ireland	6. Netherlands
7. Denmark	7. Austria	7. Austria	7. Austria	7. Denmark
8. New Zealand	8. Australia	8. Australia	8. Iceland	8. Austria
9. Netherlands	9. Belgium	9. Japan	9. Denmark	9. Ireland
10. Belgium	10. Denmark	10. Denmark	10. Canada	10. Sweden
11. Germany	11. Netherlands	11. Belgium	11. Sweden	11. Canada
12. Austria	12. Germany	12. Germany	12. Australia	12. Belgium
13. Iceland	13. Norway	13. Norway	13. Belgium	13. Germany
14. France	14. France	14. Finland	14. UK	14. Finland
15. UK	15. Italy	15. Italy	15. Japan	15. Iceland
16. Italy	16. Finland	16. Netherlands	16. Germany	16. UK
17. Finland	17. Japan	17. France	17. Italy	17. France
18. Norway	18. New Zealand	18. UK	18. Finland	18. Japan
19. Japan	19. UK	19. New Zealand	19. France	19. Italy
20. Greece	20. Greece	20. Spain	20. Israel	20. Spain

Source: OECD Statistical Extract and own calculations. Ranking based on level of living standards measured as GDP per capita.

During recent decades, Nordic nations have implemented major market liberalisations to compensate for the growth-inhibiting effects of taxes and labour market policies. Indeed, Denmark has even moved towards a flexible labour market. One reason for this is that the countries have learned their lessons from the failures of socialism.

Today few, even among the hard left, openly point to the Nordic third-way policies as a positive experience. In the 2015 edition of the Economic Freedom of the World Index, Denmark was ranked as the 11th freest economy in the world, one place above the US and two above the UK. Finland is the 19th freest economy, followed by Sweden at 23 and Norway at 27 (Heritage Foundation and *Wall Street Journal*).

Denmark stands out as having an unusually high tax share of GDP as well as uniquely market-friendly regulations. But opening up markets does not fully compensate for the effect of high taxation. Such policies affect the living standard of the average Dane. An analysis by Danish think tank CEPOS shows that increased taxes have crowded out direct household spending. Therefore the private spending of the average Danish citizen dropped from being the 6th highest in the world in 1970 to being the 14th highest in 2011. Sweden experienced a fall from 8th to 16th position during the same period (Hansen 2012). Even after the normalisation of Nordic policies, the effects of high taxes and burdensome regulations on entrepreneurship are evident.

One measure of high-impact entrepreneurship is to look at how many entrepreneurs have earned a billion-dollar fortune by creating or expanding a business. Together with Tino Sanandaji, I have worked on constructing this measure by looking at the individuals who have appeared in *Forbes* magazine's list of the world's richest people. We find that, in Scandinavian countries, the rate of high-impact entrepreneurship per capita is almost one-third that of countries with an Anglo-Saxon legal system. Political barriers have reduced the rate of successful firm creation in otherwise knowledge-intensive and innovative countries (see also Sanandaji and Sanandaji 2014).

It is important to realise that the shift towards a big state did not only end the golden entrepreneurial age while reducing economic growth. Another effect was the crowding out of private sector job creation.

4 JOB CREATION DURING FREE-MARKET AND THIRD-WAY PERIODS

Sweden is the world champion in 'jobless growth'

> Headline of article in the Swedish
> business daily *Dagens Industri* (2006)

Increasing the size of government is often, at least in the short term, a popular policy because new opportunities are created for those who directly or indirectly work with or benefit from government activities. There are of course also costs associated with expanding government but these costs typically manifest themselves in the medium or long term.

A study by economists Olivier Blanchard and Roberto Perotti, for example, focuses on how government spending and taxes affect the economy. In accordance with Keynesian theory, increased government spending is shown to lead to higher output. However, the two researchers also demonstrate that, when government increases spending and/or taxes, there is a strong negative effect on private investment (Blanchard and Perotti 2002). Cohen et al. (2011: 2) similarly show that government spending shocks appear to 'significantly dampen corporate sector investment and employment activity'. They conclude that the crowding-out effect 'suggests new considerations in assessing the impact of government spending on private sector economic activity.'

Public and private sector job growth

As discussed in the previous chapter, the transition towards an extensive welfare state reduced entrepreneurship in Sweden. Higher taxes and more regulation decreased the incentives related to creating and expanding private businesses. The same policies also led to a significant crowding out of private job growth.

Between 1950 and 2000, the Swedish population grew from seven to almost nine million. But astonishingly the net job creation in the private sector was close to zero (see Figure 3). Jobs in the public sector expanded significantly

Figure 3   Public sector and private sector cumulative net job creation (thousands) from 1950

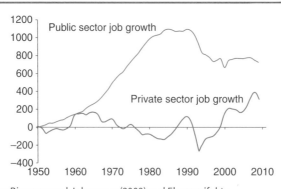

Source: Bjuggren and Johansson (2009) and Ekonomifakta.

until the end of the 1970s. After this point it became difficult to further expand the already large public sector – simply because taxes had already reached such a high level that it was not plausible to raise them further. When the welfare state could grow no larger, overall job creation came to a halt – neither the private sector nor the public sector expanded. Private sector job growth did finally occur from the 1990s following wide-ranging economic liberalisation (Bjuggren and Johansson 2009; Ekonomifakta).

The lack of job creation which resulted from the shift towards a large public sector fundamentally changed the political landscape in Sweden. Since the beginning of the 1990s the policy debate has been focused on reducing exclusion from the job market. The reason is that around one million Swedes of working age became trapped in visible and hidden unemployment. Although reforms such as tax reductions have had some success, the labour market exclusion persists. The situation is quite similar in the other Nordic nations.

Denmark has become a world leader when it comes to high tax rates. Uniquely among the Nordic nations, Denmark has a low level of labour market regulation which helps to keep unemployment low. However, it is still evident that the high levies have crowded out economic activity. Besides affecting employment, taxes can also affect the number of hours worked per individual (Ohanian et al. 2008). It is difficult to find a country that better illustrates the latter effect than Denmark does.

One study shows that as taxes rose between 1950 and 1997, average annual working hours in Danish industry dropped by 32 per cent. This can be compared with a fall of 17 per cent in Sweden and a marginal rise in hours worked in the US. Between 1950 and 1998 employment in Denmark grew by 600,000, due to population increase and the entry of women into the labour market. Despite this rise in the working population, the total number of hours worked actually fell by 10 per cent (Danish Employers' Confederation 1999). High taxes and generous welfare systems encourage individuals to work fewer hours, and less intensely, than they otherwise would.

The tale of two depressions

Sweden has long combined high taxes with rigid labour regulations that reduce the opportunities for outsiders to find work (although both areas have been reformed lately). These policies have created substantial insider–outsider effects. Even before the global financial crises, a fifth of the working-age population in Sweden was supported by some form of public benefit (Statistics Sweden 2013a).[1] A way to illustrate the effect of welfare state policies on the labour market is to look at two major crises which struck the country. One crisis occurred during the period when Sweden was characterised by low taxes and free markets. The other struck when the nation was instead characterised by high taxes and a large public sector.

---

1   This figure is given for 2006 as full-year equivalents, which means that two individuals who were on sick leave half the year each count as one individual living on benefits rather than work during that year.

The Great Depression

The first crisis was the Great Depression. As a trade-dependent nation, Sweden was not only hurt by the global economic depression, but also by the trade barriers other nations put up in a misguided effort to protect their economies from the downturn. From 1930 to 1933, the number of job opportunities available in Sweden decreased by 170,000 – one in every sixteen jobs in the economy were lost. The crisis could have been severe, especially since it occurred at the same time as many young Swedes were entering the labour force. But the Great Depression was short-lived in Sweden. Job creation soon outpaced job destruction in the dynamic economy. As is shown in Figure 4, more Swedes were working in 1935 than before the crisis (Krantz 1997).

Figure 4   Employment in Sweden (thousands) before and after the Great Depression

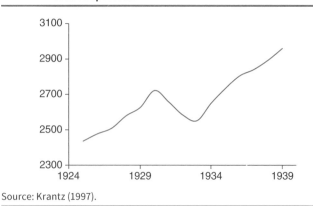

Source: Krantz (1997).

The dramatic recovery was made possible by new innovative businesses. During the crisis years, Nohab Flight engines (today known as Volvo Aero), was born. Shortly after the crisis, Securitas and SAAB were founded. A new method for creating paper pulp was invented, leading to the creation of Sunds Defibrator (today Metso Paper, a leading developer of paper industry equipment). Sweden continues to rely heavily on businesses started during or shortly after the Great Depression (see, for example, Johnson 2006). Huge opportunities were created during the Great Depression across the Nordics – illustrating the benefits of combining the Nordic culture of success with free-market systems. As Norwegian economist Ola Honningdal Grytten (2008: 379) puts it:

> During the years of depression, entrepreneurs had to come up with new innovations in order to survive. New technology was utilised in the manufacturing industry. Production became more efficient and was better matched with the actual demand. Nordic manufacturing industry was by this time able to operate in larger markets. In addition, cost-efficient production gave competitive advantage to Nordic companies. Thus, exports increased and import substitution took place.

Grytten notes that the four Nordic nations faced a significant decrease in GDP and a corresponding increase in unemployment during the Great Depression. 'However, the crisis was milder and shorter than in most other Western economies at the time, i.e. GDP and prices fell less and the

Figure 5   Unemployment in Nordic nations (per cent) before and after the Great Depression

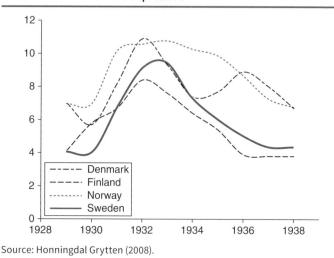

Source: Honningdal Grytten (2008).

recovery was faster.' He concludes that the labour supply of the Nordic nations rose at the same time as the depression reduced available jobs. Therefore a rise in total unemployment was observed. But this was lower than the average of other industrialised countries (ibid.: 370).

Unemployment during this period is shown in Figure 5. Given that the Nordic nations are all strongly trade-dependent, one could have expected them to be deeply hurt by the Great Depression. However, particularly Finland and Sweden reduced unemployment rapidly through new job creation from 1932 to 1933. One reason for the quick recovery was that the Nordic nations at the time had economic policies based on low taxes and liberal regulations.

Figure 6   Employment in Sweden (thousands) before and after the 1990s crisis

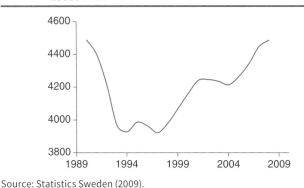

Source: Statistics Sweden (2009).

The Swedish Depression

The beginning of the 1990s saw a banking crisis hit the Swedish economy. At a time when unemployment was falling in many other countries, it rose rapidly in Sweden. Employment fell by 12 per cent between 1990 and 1993. Even when the country returned to economic growth, the employment rate rose slowly. In fact, as shown in Figure 6, it took until 2008 until it had reached the pre-1990 level – ironically, the same year that a major global crisis hit the world (Statistics Sweden 2009).

Sweden's employment rate actually fell by 0.4 per cent annually between 1992 and 2003. A McKinsey report discussed the paradox of why such a development could occur at a time when the country was experiencing strong growth. The report reached the conclusion that a poor policy environment had been hindering development: 'Labor market barriers are the main reason for the private service sector's failure to create new jobs. High taxes on employment raise the cost of labor for all employers and make low value-added services – undertaken, for instance, by restaurants, retailers, cleaning firms, and builders – very expensive' (McKinsey Quarterly 2006: 6).

Hiding unemployment

The McKinsey report also showed that, while official unemployment in Sweden was somewhat above 5 per cent in 2004, this figure was quite misleading. Much of the true unemployment was hidden by counting people as employed who were on various government programmes or by excluding some people from the unemployment figures who could work but did not find jobs. The report notes that the government at the time only counted 239,000 individuals as unemployed but that, additionally, 106,000 people were on government labour market programmes. There were also 140,000 so-called latent job candidates, individuals who were classified as not being in the labour force but who wanted to work and could start working within 14 days (e.g. full-time students who would rather work). Including these groups, the unemployment number would have risen to 485,000 (10 per cent of the labour force). Additionally, Sweden had 132,000 underemployed individuals and 215,000 people able to work but excluded from the official labour force statistics. The latter figure included people in early retirement or on prolonged sick leave beyond Sweden's normal historic levels from the

1970s. Adding all the above groups, the total unemployment figure was found to be fully 832,000, or 17 per cent of the labour force (ibid.).[2]

Although many Western countries have similar problems with labour market statistics, any long-term analysis of unemployment should take account of the much more lax definitions of 'employment' and 'looking for work' that are often used by governments when presenting unemployment statistics today. Economist Thomas Sargent, who was awarded the Nobel Prize in Economics in 2011, has co-authored a study together with economist Lars Ljungqvist in which they calculate the real underlying rate of unemployment in Sweden. The authors use historical data to sort out how much of sick leave, early retirement, etc., can be explained by hidden unemployment and overuse of welfare (Ljungqvist and Sargent 2006). In a 2014 study, Susanne Spector updates this measure. She shows that the true unemployment level in Sweden has varied between 14 and 18 per cent since 1996. In 2013, the latest available year, it was 14 per cent compared with the official statistic of 8 per cent.

Finland also went through an economic crisis during the beginning of the 1990s. According to researchers Seppo Honkapohja and Erkki Koskela, the crisis can be understood as 'a story of bad luck and bad policies'. The bad luck was due to the collapse of the Soviet Union, an important trade partner for Finland. The bad policies included

2   This figure might be an over-estimation. In particular, it is not clear how students who would rather work but continue to study since they cannot find work should be classified.

an unreformed tax system favouring debt finance and bad financial regulations. In response to the crisis, taxes rose. Together with high levels of debt among Finnish firms, this slowed down the recovery. The authors draw the conclusion: 'In the absence of bad policies, Finland would have experienced a recession, not a depression' (Honkapohja and Koskela 1999: 423).

Summing up the experience from the respective crises faced by Finland and Sweden during the 1990s, Klas Fregert and Jaakko Pehkonen write that institutional factors explain why the recovery from the crises was sluggish for both nations. It seems that increases in tax rates following the crisis raised unemployment in the two Nordic neighbours. During the following years, reforms were introduced in both countries which helped recovery. These included reduced generosity in unemployment benefits, tax reforms and less union dominance over the labour market. The reforms resulted in a substantial decrease in unemployment (Fregert and Pehkonen 2008).

Many of the obstacles to entrepreneurship and job creation still persist in both countries. In its economic survey of Finland in 2013, the OECD observed: 'In spite of substantial income tax changes in the past years, marginal tax wedges on labour income remain high, hampering incentives in labour utilisation [sic].' The organisation further remarked: 'rigidities in the labour market are hampering the smooth reallocation of the workforce from less to more productive sectors. In addition, insufficient activation of unemployed workers and high unemployment benefits are holding back employment' (OECD 2013: 11 and 8, respectively). The

OECD even recommends that oil-rich Norway implement reforms of the welfare state in order to create a better labour market, including reducing relative benefit levels and making it more difficult to overuse the disability benefits system (OECD 2012a).

Regardless of the label we use to describe Nordic economies in the 1970s, the conclusion is the same: the systems were not nearly as successful in creating prosperity, successful entrepreneurial firms and new jobs as the Nordic free-market model of the first half of the same century had been.

5 HIDING THE RISE OF TAXATION

Fiscal illusion distorts democratic decisions and may result in 'excessive' redistribution.

Jean-Robert Tyran and Rupert Sausgruber (2005: 49)

It is sometimes puzzling to the outsider why the Nordic public have repeatedly elected tax-raising governments to power. The obvious answer is ideological support for welfare state policies. However, there is another reason: the general public has not been fully aware of the price tag, in terms of higher taxes, attached to expanding public sectors. Politicians have created a 'fiscal illusion' which has resulted in higher levels of taxation than the population would otherwise have accepted as feasible had taxes been levied in a transparent way.

Before policies radicalised in the late 1960s, the tax levels in Nordic nations were around 30 per cent of GDP – quite typical of other developed nations. At the time, the tax burdens were quite visible. Most taxation occurred through direct taxes, which showed up on employees' payslips. Over time, an increasing share of taxation has been raised through indirect taxes. The latter are less visible to those paying them, since they are either levied before

Figure 7   Hidden and visible taxes in Finland (percentage of GDP)

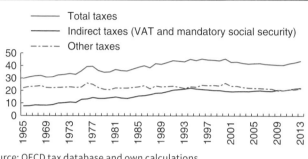

Source: OECD tax database and own calculations.

the wage is formally given to the employee or are included in the listed price of goods.

Finland is worth considering as an example. The country's tax level was 30 per cent of GDP in 1965. Indirect taxes in the form of VAT and mandatory social security contributions amounted to 8 per cent of GDP. In 2013 the total tax take had increased to 44 per cent of GDP, while indirect taxes had risen 22 per cent (see Figure 7); in Denmark the total tax take rose from 30 to 49 per cent of GDP, while indirect taxation increased from 4 to 10 per cent (Figure 8); in Norway the corresponding figures are 30 and 41 per cent for total taxation and 4 and 18 per cent for indirect taxation (Figure 9); lastly in Sweden the total level of taxation rose from 31 to 43 per cent of GDP while indirect taxation went from 4 to 19 per cent (Figure 10).[1]

---

1   OECD tax database and own calculations. For the sake of simplicity, indirect taxes include only the VAT and mandatory social security contributions. This significantly under-estimates the level of hidden taxation as minor hidden taxes such as those on alcohol, power generation and payroll

Figure 8 Hidden and visible taxes in Denmark (percentage of GDP)

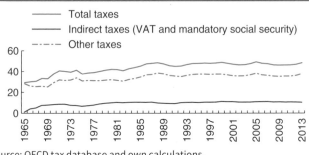

Source: OECD tax database and own calculations.

In other words, except in Denmark, visible taxes have reduced over the period while the total tax burden has significantly increased. This is in line with the predictions of fiscal illusion made by Italian economist Amilcare Puviani in 1903. Puviani explained that politicians would have incentives to hide the cost of government by levying indirect rather than direct taxes, so that the public would under-estimate the cost of policies. The illusion can thus be created that an expanding state benefits individuals and families and yet costs less than it actually does (Baker 1983). Nobel laureate James Buchanan and other researchers have expanded on the idea that it is easier for politicians to raise hidden, indirect taxes rather than visible ones (see, for example, Buchanan 1960; Baker 1983).

One example of a hidden indirect tax is that of 'employers' fees' or employers' social security contributions. These

taxes are not included. Detailed OECD data are available from 1965 and onward and thus this is chosen as the start year. For Denmark, slightly different data are available and so the base year of 1966 has been used and the figures are partly derived from the author's own calculations.

Figure 9   Hidden and visible taxes in Norway (percentage of GDP)

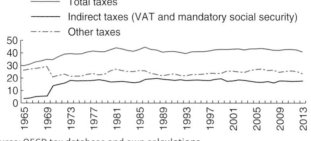

Source: OECD tax database and own calculations.

Figure 10 Hidden and visible taxes in Sweden (percentage of GDP)

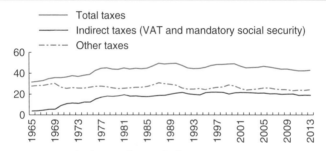

Source: OECD tax database and own calculations.

are levied on the employer rather than the employee and thus are invisible to the electorate. However, the effect of these taxes is broadly similar to the effect of direct taxation of employees.

In a survey conducted in 2003, the Swedish public was asked to estimate the total amount of taxes they paid. The respondents were reminded to include all forms of direct and indirect taxation. Almost half of the respondents believed that the total taxes amounted to around 30–35 per cent of their income. At the time of the survey, the total tax rate levied on an average income earner, including consumption taxes, was around 60 per cent (described in Sanandaji and Wallace (2011)). Other more recent studies strengthen the notion that many Swedes are unaware of the extent of hidden taxes levied on their incomes (see, for example, Larsson 2009). This is in line with international studies about indirect taxation. Jean-Robert Tyran and Rupert Sausgruber, for example, show that 'tax burden associated with an indirect tax is systematically under-estimated, whereas this is not the case with an equivalent direct tax' (Tyran and Sausgruber 2005: 39).

To summarise, the design of Nordic tax systems has over time created a 'fiscal illusion', whereby the public is not aware of the taxes they are paying. One can reflect on whether it is really in line with democratic principles to raise taxes in a way such that citizens are unaware of them. Interestingly, few proponents of introducing a Nordic model of high taxes in other countries stress that such a move would require hiding the true cost of taxation from the public.

Scandinavian countries would be even more prosperous with lower taxes

A common perception is that Nordic nations have stum-bled over a secret recipe, in which high taxes have little if any negative consequences. This does not find support in the research. Numerous studies have shown that the high levels of taxation are damaging to the Nordic economies. Hidden or not, the tax burden matters.

A study published by the European Central Bank, for example, finds that Sweden is on the tip of the Laffer curve when it comes to average taxes on incomes. This means that increasing taxes further on labour would have such a damaging effect on the economy that revenues would not increase. Tax rates in Denmark and Finland are also shown to be close to this extreme case (Norway is not included in the analysis). For capital taxation, Denmark and Sweden are shown to be on the wrong side of the Laffer curve. This means that capital taxes in the two countries are so damaging that reducing them would actually lead to more money being collected by the tax authorities (Trabandt and Uhlig 2010).

Several other studies support the idea that Swedish taxes are at, or close to, the tip of the Laffer curve (see, for example, Holmlund and Söderström 2007). For instance, economist Åsa Hansson calculates the efficiency loss for each additional Swedish krona levied and spent by the government. This loss can, according to Hansson, be up to three additional krona if the money is spent on welfare payments which reduce the incentives for work (Hansson 2009).

To understand why taxes can have such significantly negative effects on the economy, one can consider the situation of a Swedish worker paying the maximum marginal tax rate and consuming his earnings. A payroll tax of 32 per cent is paid on the gross wage. There is then an average municipal tax of 32 per cent and a state tax of 25 per cent. Finally, there is an average consumption tax of 21 per cent. A government report has calculated that the total effective marginal tax rate is 73 per cent. This is above the estimate of the top of the Laffer curve in the same report, indicating again that a lower tax rate could in fact lead to higher public revenues (Pirttilä and Selin 2011).

A number of Danish studies point in the same direction. The think tank CEPOS in Copenhagen has, for example, calculated the effects of reducing the top marginal tax rate on labour from 56 to 40 per cent.[2] The total effect of increased working hours among the affected groups would correspond to adding between 20,000 to 55,000 extra individuals to the labour force (Lundby Hansen 2011).

Lastly, it is important to bear in mind that the estimates relating to the effect of taxes are based on short-term and medium-term consequences. Economic research supports the notion that taxes also affect long-term decisions, relating to choice of career, investment in education and the number of hours worked (see, for example, Ohanian et al. (2008) as well as Rogerson (2009)). The long-term benefits of tax cuts in the Nordics are likely to be even greater than the above-mentioned estimates indicate.

The popular notion that high taxes have not impaired economic development in Nordic nations is simply not true. Affluent Nordic nations would be even more affluent with a lower tax burden.

---

2   These are the rates excluding indirect taxes.

6 ADMIRABLE SOCIAL OUTCOMES AND LOW LEVELS OF INEQUALITY BEFORE BIG WELFARE STATES

> On any measure of the health of a society – from economic indicators like productivity and innovation to social ones like inequality and crime – the Nordic countries are gathered near the top.
>
> *The Economist* (2013a)

The Nordic states adopted welfare policies during the first half of the 20th century. Initially, however, the welfare institutions were financed by relatively low taxes. Even in 1960, for example, tax revenues amounted to 25 per cent of GDP in Denmark, 28 per cent in Finland, 29 per cent in Sweden and 32 per cent in Norway. This can be compared with rates of 27 per cent of GDP in the UK and 34 per cent in Germany at the same time (The Swedish Tax Agency 2007). A key point is that before the Nordic nations had large welfare states they also exhibited good social outcomes.

In Table 5 life expectancy at birth is shown for various OECD nations in 1960. Norway had the highest life expectancy, followed by Sweden, Iceland and Denmark in third to fifth positions. Finland was in 22nd position.

Table 5 Life expectancy at birth in 1960

1	Norway	73.6
2	Netherlands	73.5
3	Sweden	73.1
4	Iceland	72.8
5	Denmark	72.4
6	Switzerland	71.6
7	Canada	71.3
8	New Zealand	71.3
9	Australia	70.9
10	UK	70.8
22	Finland	69.0

Source: Wallen and Fölster (2009).

Table 6 Life expectancy at birth in 2005

1	Japan	82.1
2	Switzerland	81.3
3	Iceland	81.2
4	Australia	80.9
5	Spain	80.7
6	Sweden	80.6
7	Italy	80.4
8	France	80.3
9	Canada	80.2
10	Norway	80.1
17	UK	79.0
18	Finland	78.9
22	Denmark	77.9

Source: Wallen and Fölster (2009).

The corresponding ranking is shown for the year 2005 in Table 6, before the financial crisis and after the transition from small welfare states supported by relatively low taxes to large welfare states supported by high taxes.

In 2005 the Nordic nations were still characterised by relatively long life expectancy. However, if anything they had fallen somewhat behind the rest of the world.[1] The gap in life expectancy between the UK and the average Nordic nation had been 1.2 years in 1960. In 2005 it had shrunk to a third of that level. The gap to the US had gone from 2.2 to

---

1   Finland is the exception, since Finland was very poor after World War II and grew rich afterwards.

1.6 years. This simple comparison illustrates the need to separate correlation from causation. High life expectancy was not simply caused by large welfare states.[2]

The argument for adopting a Nordic economic model as suggested by the left is straightforward: life expectancy and other social outcomes are good in this region; therefore, if Nordic tax and welfare policies are adopted in the UK or the US, the same result will emerge there. But any deeper analysis shows that these good outcomes existed before the introduction of Nordic tax and welfare policies.

Iceland has smaller government, but better social outcomes

Equally interesting is the case of Iceland. In 1960 the life expectancy in Iceland was below that of Norway and Sweden, and higher than that of Denmark and Finland. In 2005 Iceland had better life expectancy than all the major Scandinavian countries. This was despite the fact that Iceland deviates from the larger Scandinavian countries by having a moderate welfare model, supported by a tax take of around 36 per cent of GDP.[3] In 2011 the life expectancy

---

2   The trends are similar in more recent life-span data from 2011. Switzerland ranks at the top, followed by Japan and Iceland. Sweden ranks 7th, Norway 10th and Finland and Denmark have positions 23 and 26 respectively. The Nordics have thus fallen behind even more in life expectancy. Source: World Bank Database.

3   OECD tax database. This was the average tax take in Iceland between 2003 and 2013. The corresponding figure is 42 per cent in Finland, 43 in Norway, 44 in Sweden and 47 in Denmark.

in Iceland was 82.4 years, compared with 81.8 in Sweden, 81.3 in Norway, 80.5 in Finland and 79.8 in Denmark (World Bank Database). Evidently, a moderately sized public sector can be combined with long life expectancy in Scandinavia.

High life expectancy is certainly not simply 'caused' by large welfare states. Even before their welfare states expanded, Nordic societies could benefit from high incomes, strong social norms and cohesion as well as a love for nature and sport. Some of these advantages are to do with the Nordic way of life, rather than policy. The lifestyle advantages still persist, both in Iceland, which still has a moderately sized public sector, and in the larger Scandinavian countries, which have more extensive welfare policies.

The fact that Denmark fell so much behind Sweden between 1960 and 2005 in terms of life expectancy relates to differences in lifestyle. The Danes are famous for enjoying life more than their Nordic cousins. This goes hand in hand with high rates of alcohol consumption and smoking. Today Danes live shorter lives than Swedes. That Denmark has surpassed its northern neighbour in terms of the level of taxes does not change this fact. A simplistic idealisation of Scandinavian social democracy simply fails to capture the true roots of societal features. The comparisons of the rate of child mortality point in the same direction (Tables 7 and 8). Again, Sweden had the second lowest global rates in 2005. But it also had the second lowest rates in 1960. In both years Iceland was ranked as having the lowest child mortality in the world. The latest data from 2013 shows

Table 7 Infant mortality in 1960 (per thousand)		
1	Iceland	13.1
2	Sweden	16.6
3	Netherlands	17.9
4	Norway	18.9
5	Czech Republic	20.0
6	Australia	20.2
7	Finland	21.0
8	Switzerland	21.1
9	Denmark	21.5
10	UK	22.5

Source: Wallen and Fölster (2009).

Table 8 Infant mortality in 2005 (per thousand)		
1	Iceland	2.3
2	Sweden	2.4
3	Luxembourg	2.6
4	Japan	2.8
5	Finland	3.0
6	Norway	3.1
7	Czech Republic	3.4
8	Portugal	3.5
9	France	3.6
10	Belgium	3.7
17	Denmark	4.4
22	UK	5.1

Source: Wallen and Fölster (2009).

that the infant mortality rate per thousand is 1.6 in Iceland, 2.1 in Finland, 2.3 in Norway, 2.4 in Sweden and 2.9 in Denmark (CME data). Iceland continues to lie ahead.

The point is not to argue that Nordic societies are not successful. Clearly they are. The point is that Nordic success is not directly the result of large welfare states and high tax rates. The recipe for success is either to be found in cultural characteristics that have long set these countries apart or, alternatively, in the particular design of welfare policies which worked well before Nordic welfare states became larger than those in other European or Anglo-Saxon countries. The case of Iceland, as well as the historical comparison, strongly supports this conclusion.

Egalitarian income distribution before big government

Nordic nations are admired by policymakers in other nations for a range of social outcomes. Perhaps the most important one is an even income distribution. However, counter-intuitively, this also predates the big welfare state – certainly in Sweden and Denmark.

A comparison of historical rates of income inequality in Sweden, the US, Canada, France and Netherlands shows interesting results. By 1920, well before the existence of a large-scale welfare state, Sweden had among the lowest levels of inequality within this group of countries. The authors of the study, economists Jesper Roine and Daniel Waldenström, note the following regarding the evolution of top income shares in Sweden during the period between 1903 and 2004: 'We find that, starting from levels of inequality approximately equal to those in other Western countries at the time, the income share of the Swedish top decile drops sharply over the first eighty years of the twentieth century. Most of the decrease takes place before the expansion of the welfare state and by 1950 Swedish top income shares were already lower than in other countries' (Roine and Waldenstrom 2008: 366).

A recent paper by Anthony Barnes Atkinson and Jakob Egholt Søgaard illustrates that the evolution towards greater equality of incomes in Denmark followed a similar route. The paper shows that the Gini coefficient of taxable income moved considerably towards higher levels of equality during the last three decades of the 19th century as well as in the first half of the 20th century. Most of the shift towards higher equality happened before the introduction of a large public sector and high taxes (Atkinson and Søgaard 2013).

The same paper compares the top 10 per cent income shares in Denmark, Sweden and Norway. In all three countries the share dropped markedly between 1900 and 1970; it continued to fall somewhat until the mid-1980s, and has since increased again to the levels around 1970. A similar trend can be shown for the incomes of the top 1 per cent. Again, the changes mostly occurred before the shift towards high taxes (ibid.). Tino Sanandaji argues in another study: 'American scholars who write about the success of the Scandinavian welfare states in the postwar period tend to be remarkably uninterested in Scandinavia's history prior to that period. Scandinavia was likely the most egalitarian part of Europe even before the modern era. For example, it was the only major part of Western Europe that never developed full-scale feudalism and never reduced its farmers to serfdom' (Sanandaji 2012b: 56–57).

Welfare policies and taxes, do, of course, affect income distribution. Part of the rise in income equality in Nordic nations is most likely to be due to the introduction of large welfare systems. However, other factors have clearly also played a vital role and egalitarianism long predates the welfare state. One of these factors is the Nordic culture of success, built upon a strong work ethic and social cohesion. Another is a broad base of wealth creation within the market-based systems. Well-functioning early welfare institutions, introduced when taxes were still low, also fostered equal opportunities.

What is not as clear is the role played by extensive government welfare payments and high taxes. The direct effect of such policies is of course to create more equality. But an indirect long-term consequence is that some of those with lower productivity are locked out of the labour market, instead becoming dependent on welfare payments. This effect, which will be discussed below, is quite evident in the Nordics.

Which countries have even income and wealth distributions?

If we look at the European nations that have the most even income distributions, we do not only find the Nordic nations, but also Slovenia, the Czech Republic and Slovakia at the top (Table 9). The latter three countries certainly do not have a Nordic model. They have lower, and in the case of the Czech Republic flat, taxes. What they do have in common with the Nordic nations is homogeneous populations.

When the vast majority of the citizens of a country share the same culture, their incomes are likely to be more similar than in countries with big differences in culture. One of the reasons that children's incomes are related to those of their parents is that general differences exist between subgroups within society.[4] High levels of homogeneity are a key factor behind the high equality in the Nordic nations. It is also an important explanation for why

---

4   Studies that have decomposed mobility find that more than half of the intergenerational correlation in the United States is due to persistence of earnings differences across racial and ethnic groups. See Hertz (2008).

Table 9   Gini coefficient of disposable incomes

Iceland	0.244	Sweden	0.269	Canada	0.320
Slovenia	0.246	Luxembourg	0.270	Greece	0.337
Norway	0.249	Germany	0.286	Spain	0.338
Denmark	0.252	Netherlands	0.288	UK	0.341
Czech Republic	0.256	France	0.303	Portugal	0.344
Finland	0.260	Poland	0.305	Israel	0.376
Slovak Republic	0.261	Korea	0.310	US	0.380
Belgium	0.262	Estonia	0.319	Mexico	0.466
Austria	0.267	Italy	0.319		

Source: OECD Stat Extract, 2010 figures. Incomes post taxes and transfers are used for the calculation.

income equality is so much harder to achieve in heterogeneous nations such as the US, or even the UK. Indeed, part of the increase in income inequality which has occurred in Scandinavian countries during the last few decades relates to the inflow of immigrants. Through immigration Nordic countries have become less homogeneous and thus more unequal. Looking at Table 9, it is evident that Iceland has the most equal income distribution, ahead of both Slovenia and the four larger Scandinavian countries.

Finally, it is worth looking at wealth inequality. One might expect Nordic nations to have high levels of wealth equality. But, as the first results from the Luxembourg Wealth Study indicate (Table 10), this is not necessarily the case. A comparison between seven different industrial nations shows that Italy and the UK have relatively high levels of wealth equality, at least among the small group

Table 10 Gini coefficient of wealth distribution

Italy	61
UK	66
Finland	68
Canada	75
Germany	78
US	81–84*
Sweden	89

* Two different estimates are calculated for the US.
Source: Brandolini et al. (2008).

of nations included in the study. Finland ranks in third place, followed by Canada and Germany. The US has the second lowest wealth equality. Surprisingly, Sweden exhibits the highest level of wealth inequality (Brandolini et al. 2008).

The reason for this uniquely uneven wealth distribution is that many Swedish households depend on government safety nets and thus have limited savings. A study in 2009 showed that around 30 per cent of Swedish households had negative, or zero, assets. Around 20 per cent had asset levels that corresponded to around one month's salary for a normal household (Skattebetalarnas Förening 2009). The welfare state has certainly promoted more even income distribution. But it has also led to a situation where the homogeneous Swedish society has become characterised by vast differences in private wealth.

7 SUCCESS OF SCANDINAVIAN DESCENDANTS IN THE US

A Scandinavian economist once said to Milton Friedman: 'In Scandinavia, we have no poverty.' Milton Friedman replied: 'That's interesting, because in America, among Scandinavians, we have no poverty, either.'

Quoted by Kotkin (2009)

The descendants of Scandinavian migrants on the other side of the Atlantic live in a very different policy environment compared with the residents of the Scandinavian countries. The former live in an environment with less welfare, lower taxes and (in general) freer markets. Interestingly, the social and economic success of the descendants of Scandinavian migrants in the US is on a par with or even better than their cousins in Scandinavia.[1]

---

1 Some of the facts and arguments in this chapter appeared in a column David Brooks published in the *New York Times* on 3 May 2010. It should be noted that the author of this book coauthored an article with the same statistics and arguments in the *New Geography* on the day before the publication of Mr Brooks's article. The two articles are included in the footnotes. See *New Geography* (2010) and *New York Times* (2010).

Nordic societies have for hundreds of years benefited from sound institutions, a strong Lutheran work ethic and high levels of trust and civic participation. These cultural phenomena do not disappear when Nordic people cross the Atlantic. On the contrary, they appear to bloom fully. Close to 12 million Americans have Scandinavian origins, that is to say are individuals whose ancestors largely or in some cases entirely migrated from Scandinavia and who today identify as having Scandinavian origins. This group is characterised by favourable social and economic outcomes. According to the 2010 US Census, the median household income in the United States is $51,914. This can be compared with a median household income of $61,920 for Danish Americans, $59,379 for Finnish-Americans, $60,935 for Norwegian Americans and $61,549 for Swedish Americans. There is also a group identifying themselves simply as 'Scandinavian Americans' in the US Census. The median household income for this group is even higher at $66,219 (US Census database).

It is notable that Norwegian Americans have household incomes 17 per cent higher than the US average. If we assume that their contribution to GDP is also 17 per cent higher, the GDP per capita of Norwegian Americans would amount to $55,396. This is only slightly less than the $57,945 GDP per capita of oil-rich Norway. Corresponding calculations show that Danish Americans have a contribution to GDP per capita 37 per cent higher than Danes still living in Denmark; Swedish Americans contribute 39 per cent more to GDP per capita than Swedes living in Sweden; and Finnish Americans contribute 47 per cent more than

Finns living in Finland. We cannot draw definitive conclusions from these figures, since household composition may differ, but there is prima facie evidence that Scandinavians who move to the US are significantly better off than those who stay at home.

Those Scandinavians who went to the US, predominantly in the nineteenth century, were not elite groups. A recent study, for example, compared Norwegians who migrated to the US with those who stayed in Norway. The study shows that the Norwegians who moved from urban areas tended to face poorer economic conditions than those who stayed behind (Abramitzky et al. 2012).

The success of Nordic immigrants in the US shows the pervasiveness of norms and low-level social institutions. The comparison with Scandinavian Americans suggests that the pursuit to create 'social good' through welfare state policies has hindered economic prosperity. Economists Notten and Neubourg have calculated the poverty rates in European countries and the US using equivalent measures. They have shown that the absolute poverty rates in Denmark (6.7 per cent) and Sweden (9.3 per cent) are indeed lower than the US level (11 per cent). For Finland, however, the rate (15 per cent) is somewhat higher than in the US (Notten and de Neubourg 2011). At the same time, Nordic nations have, even before the rise of large welfare states, long been characterised by low levels of poverty. Nordic descendants in the US today have half the poverty rate of average Americans – a consistent finding for decades. In other words, Nordic Americans have lower poverty rates than Nordic citizens (Sanandaji 2012b).

Thus, what makes Nordics uniquely successful is not the welfare states, as is commonly assumed. Rather than being the cause of these nations' social strengths, the high-tax welfare state instead seems to have been made possible by the hard-won stock of social capital. It was well before the welfare state, when hard work paid off, that a culture with an emphasis on a work ethic and strong trust and social cohesion developed. It was these informal institutions that paved the way for the introduction of large welfare states which were buttressed by strong social norms. However, in the long run, the large welfare states eroded incentives, and ultimately the social norms that bound Scandinavian societies together.

8 WELFARE DEPENDENCY

I believe in the competition-state as the modern welfare state. If we are to ensure support for the welfare state, we must focus on the quality of public services rather than transfer payments.

> Danish social democrat Finance Minister
> Bjarne Corydon, on the need to reduce
> the generosity of transfer systems,
> in the Danish paper *Politiken* (2013)

As discussed earlier, the expansion of the Scandinavian welfare states has led to a crowding out of private sector job creation. It has also coincided with an increase in the share of the population who are supported by various forms of government transfers. Initially, the Nordic welfare states were focused on providing various services to their citizens. Tax funds were spent on infrastructure, schooling and health. Safety nets did exist, but few used them. Over time, an increasing share of the population became dependent on government transfers. The welfare states moved from offering services to the broad public to transferring benefits to those who did not work.

Dependence on benefits

Since the beginning of the 1990s, approximately one-fifth of the Swedish population of working age has been supported by unemployment benefits, sick leave benefits or early retirement benefits. This was a conclusion reached by Jan Edling in 2005. Interestingly, Edling wrote his original analysis of the high hidden unemployment, and its connection with the overuse of welfare services, while working as an analyst for the Swedish Trade Union Confederation (LO) (Edling 2005).

The confederation has very close ties to the Swedish social democratic party, which at the time controlled the government. The Swedish Trade Union Confederation refused to publish the report, believing it to be critical of the government in particular and the social democratic welfare model in general. Edling quit his job in protest and made the material publicly available. Other studies have since supported the findings about high levels of hidden unemployment (see, for example, Confederation of Swedish Enterprise 2006; Herin et al. 2006; Edling 2010).

The debate that followed has changed the perspective on welfare policies in the country. Support for the welfare state remains strong. At the same time, there is today a general understanding that rigid labour regulations, high taxes and generous government benefits contribute to excluding a share of the population from the labour market.

Healthy but sick

The point of a generous welfare state is to aid individuals and families. However, the Nordic systems also foster dependency among those who could otherwise take care of their own lives. One illustration is that many who are long-term unemployed are classified as early retired. Although in many cases healthy enough to work, the individuals are categorised as too sick, or disabled, to work in order to hide them from the unemployment statistics (Sanandaji 2011). This classification in itself can reduce the likelihood of individuals returning to work. The resulting exclusion not only matters for economic reasons. There is also a social aspect to consider: essentially healthy individuals become dependent on handouts and are told by the state that they are disabled. One can wonder what this does to individual self-esteem and confidence, and question whether it is a desirable outcome of welfare policy.

Nordic nations are characterised by unusually good health. Paradoxically, they are also world leaders in public spending on disability and sickness absence. A study by the OECD calculates the share of GDP that goes to incapacity-related unemployment. In Table 11, various OECD countries are ranked according to the average level for the years 1990, 2000 and 2005. Over this period the Netherlands is the only country where spending on incapacity-related unemployment has generally been higher than in Scandinavian countries.

On average 5 per cent of national income in Norway was spent on unemployment due to disability and sickness in the years shown above. The corresponding levels in Sweden and Finland were 4.4 and 3.2 per cent respectively. This can be compared with 0.4 per cent in Canada, 1.3 per cent in the US and 2.4 per cent in the UK. One reason is that expenditure for each individual is more generous in Norway, Sweden and Finland. Another is, in accordance with the observations by Edling and others, high rates of hidden unemployment.

Denmark also has expensive public programmes. However, the country differs from the other major Nordic nations by having a liberal labour market, which leads to less social exclusion. This can explain why Denmark, during the period, spent 2.9 per cent of GDP on disability and sickness – considerably less than in Sweden and Norway. The smaller Nordic country of Iceland, which also has a relatively liberal labour market, had a similar spending level of 3.0 per cent. Sickness and disability spending should relate to health status. In the Nordics it also relates to labour market exclusion, which is lower in the countries with more liberal employment regulation.

How can the young retire?

The practice of using sick leave and early retirement to hide the true unemployment rate is extended to the youth. In 2013 five representatives from The Swedish Social Insurance Inspectorate examined the share of young people (18–29-year-olds) who were supported by early retirement in the Nordics. The study shows that at the end of the 1990s around 1 per cent of the youth in Sweden, Finland and

Table 11 Spending on disability and sickness programmes as a share of GDP

	Average for 1990, 2000 and 2005	1990	2000	2005
Netherlands	5.7	7.6	4.9	4.6
Norway	5.0	5.1	5.1	4.9
Sweden	4.4	5.0	4.1	4.2
Finland	3.2	3.6	3.0	3.1
Iceland	3.0	2.3	3.1	3.6
Denmark	2.9	2.9	2.6	3.1
Switzerland	2.7	2.2	2.8	3.2
Poland	2.7	2.8	3.0	2.3
Austria	2.6	3.1	2.3	2.4
Germany	2.5	2.7	2.5	2.2
Luxembourg	2.5	2.6	2.3	2.5
United Kingdom	2.4	2.2	2.8	2.3
Australia	2.4	1.6	3.0	2.5
Belgium	2.3	2.8	1.9	2.1
Czech Republic	2.2	2.3	2.3	2.1
Spain	2.2	2.2	2.2	2.2
OECD	2.1	2.3	2.1	2.0
Portugal	1.8	1.7	1.8	1.8
Italy	1.7	2.1	1.6	1.3
France	1.6	1.6	1.5	1.6
Greece	1.5	1.9	1.4	1.3
Ireland	1.3	1.3	1.1	1.5
United States	1.3	1.3	1.2	1.4
New Zealand	1.1	0.9	1.2	1.3
Canada	0.4	0.4	0.4	0.4
Japan	0.4	0.4	0.4	0.4
Korea	0.2	0.2	0.2	0.2

Source: OECD (2009).

Denmark were supported by early retirement. By 2011, this figure rose to 1.5 per cent in Denmark and Finland and to 2 per cent in Sweden. Norway, which has the most generous welfare system, had close to 2 per cent of the youth in early retirement by the late 1990s; by 2011 the figure had climbed to 5 per cent. There are also regional variations within the Scandinavian countries. The share of youths on early retirement is higher in regions with high unemployment (Bernitz et al. 2013).[1]

The significant rise in youth early retirement has not been driven by increases in actual disability. By international standards, Nordic people have good health. Much like the rest of the world, health is improving over time due to rising prosperity and medical development. In addition modern technologies and working habits have increased the possibilities for those with disabilities to work. We should expect fewer, not more, young people to rely on early retirement. The rise over time signifies entrapment in welfare dependency.

Several different welfare systems exist in the Scandinavian countries through which the populations become dependent on benefits rather than work. Using early retirement to hide unemployment among the youth is perhaps the most perverse one. The result is that individuals are trapped in a position of social exclusion that is likely to become lifelong. Young people are given the erroneous impression that they are simply not fit to participate in society.

---

1 In Finland and Sweden the statistics also include 16- and 17-year-olds.

Policymakers in Scandinavian countries are aware that early retirement hides true unemployment. The benefit levels given to early retired youth are therefore among the least generous in the transfer systems. Of course, this makes sense in terms of ensuring incentives to work are maintained. However, it also means that those who are born with, or acquire, disabilities that prevent them from working at a young age will receive among the lowest levels of public transfers. Overuse of the system of early retirement has led to a situation where Nordic societies have in effect come to limit aid to those that truly need help (Sanandaji 2011).

Welfare dependency and social poverty

Of course, young people who have been given early retirement are a small proportion of the total excluded from the Nordic labour markets. Also for other groups, economic and social marginalisation can follow welfare dependency. As the Nobel laureate Robert Fogel has suggested, poverty exists in modern societies to a large degree because of an uneven distribution of 'spiritual resources' such as self-esteem, a sense of discipline and a sense of community (Fogel 1999). These problems are exacerbated when individuals who could otherwise be self-reliant become dependent on public support.

In Denmark, the notion that welfare policies have created overuse of and entrapment in the benefit systems is acknowledged even by the ruling social democrats. Bjarne Corydon, the country's social democrat Finance Minister, made international headlines in 2013 by discussing the need to reduce the generosity of transfer systems in the country. Corydon explained that it was no mere coincidence that the government was reforming taxes, welfare aid and the system for early retirement: 'The truth is that we are in full swing with a dramatically positive agenda, which is about strengthening and modernising the welfare state, and the result of the change will be a much better society than the one we have today' (Politiken 2013). The Danish Finance Minister's vision makes sense, even from the perspective of a social democrat. If reforms can lead to less dependency on welfare benefits, it will be possible to strengthen both economic development and the funding of welfare services such as health care or education. More importantly, social poverty will be reduced when people move towards self-reliance.

The perverse effects of welfare systems coupled with high taxes and rigid labour markets are clearly seen also in Norway. The most generous Nordic welfare system has created a class of socially poor. In the article 'The confessions of a "welfare freeloader"', published in the daily paper *Dagbladet*, a young man wrote in 2012 about how he had been supported by welfare for the last three years, although he was vital and in his prime years. In this, he was not alone: 'I know several people – talented, gifted people – who do not take a job. They do not do much else either, seen from a societal standpoint. No studies, no clearly defined plan for the future and no cunning plans to create wealth of any kind. The interest to "participate" or to "help" is minimal within this group, and poses no motivation to talk about.

The feeling of responsibility when it comes to an abstract entity as "society" is low' (*Dagbladet* 2012).

The aim of welfare states is to lift people out of poverty, to provide social security nets and basic welfare services. In many ways Scandinavian societies have succeeded in these fields. But the move from small to large welfare systems has also created social poverty, even among otherwise healthy and young individuals. This is simply not in line with the ideals of a good society. More welfare is not always better welfare.

9 THE WELFARE STATE – SOCIAL POVERTY AND ETHICAL VALUES

[T]rust is high in universal welfare states, not because welfare state universality creates trust, but because trusting populations are more likely to create and sustain large, universal welfare states

Andreas Bergh and Christian Bjørnskov (2011: 1)

For a long time, the religious, cultural and economic systems in Scandinavian societies fostered individual responsibility and a strong work ethic. These norms were important for the success of the nations as they moved towards free-market systems in the late nineteenth and early twentieth century. In addition, social democratic politicians viewed this unique culture, coupled with uniquely homogeneous societies, as the optimal starting point for expanding welfare states. Since the norms relating to work and responsibility were so strong, Nordic citizens usually did not try to avoid taxes or misuse generous public support systems in the early years. Also, 'one-size-fits-all' welfare states are typically less disruptive in a strongly homogeneous social environment, since most of the population has similar ethics, preferences and income levels.

Strong social norms opened the way for a substantial expansion of government. But, as Nordic citizens became accustomed to high taxes and generous government benefits, attitudes gradually changed. This shift is possible to track historically, by looking at the response given to the same question over several years in the World Value Survey. In this survey, individuals around the world are asked a number of questions, one of which is whether they believe it is justifiable to claim government benefits to which they are not entitled. In the 1981–84 survey, 82 per cent of Swedes and 80 per cent of Norwegians agreed with the statement 'claiming government benefits to which you are not entitled is never justifiable'.[1]

The citizens in the two countries still had a strong ethical approach to government benefits until the 1980s. However, as the population adjusted its culture to new economic policies, benefit morale dropped steadily. In the survey of 2005–8, only 56 per cent of Norwegians and 61 per cent of Swedes believed that it was never right to claim benefits to which they were not entitled. The 2010–14 survey only includes Sweden out of the Scandinavian countries. It shows that benefit morale has continued to fall in Sweden: only 55 per cent answered that it was never right to overuse benefits (ibid.).[2]

---

1   World Value Survey data. See further discussion in Heinemann (2008).

2   In Sweden the share dropped to 55 per cent in the 1999–2004 survey. The temporary rise to 61 per cent in the 2005–8 survey followed an extensive public policy debate relating to overuse of welfare services as well as significant reforms to welfare services and taxes. For Finland, reliable data from early surveys does not exist. In Denmark between the 1981–84 and

A link between government benefits and cultural transmissions of work ethics has been suggested by Jean-Baptiste Michau. In a study from 2009 he notes that parents make rational choices regarding 'how much effort to exert to raise their children to work hard', based on their 'expectations on the policy that will be implemented by the next generation'. Therefore, a significant lag should exist between the introduction of certain policies, or even a public debate regarding future policies, and changes in ethical views. Building a model with a lag between these two factors, Michau argues that generous unemployment insurance benefits can explain a substantial fraction of the history of unemployment in Europe after World War II (Michau 2009: 2).

Similarly, Swedish researchers Assar Lindbeck and Sten Nyberg find empirical support for the conclusion that: 'generous social insurance arrangements tend to weaken parents' incentives to instill [work] norms in their children' (Lindbeck and Nyberg 2006: 1473; see also Lindbeck et al. 1999). The situation that exists in Nordic societies today is one in which ethics relating to work and responsibility are not strongly encouraged by the economic systems. Individuals with low skills and education have limited gains from working. This is particularly true of parents of large families, which gain extra support if on welfare.

As an illustration, a report published by the Danish social democrat government in 2013 concluded that 400,000 Danish citizens have few economic incentives to

the 1999–2004 surveys the share fell from 92 to 83 per cent, suggesting a slower shift of norms than in Norway and Sweden.

participate in the labour market. These individuals lose 80 per cent or more of their incomes when entering the labour market, since they lose benefits and have to pay taxes. Through extensive reforms of taxes and benefits the government hopes to reduce the group to 250,000 individuals. Even this would be a large share of the working-age population, which is below 3 million (Økonomi og indenrigsministeriet 2013).[3]

In 2012 the social democratic government in Denmark started a debate about the need for individuals to take more responsibility for their own lives in the future welfare model (*Jyllands Posten* 2012). An important reason for this was changes in norms. The Danish researcher Casper Hunnerup Dahl has reached the conclusion: 'The high degree of distribution in the Danish welfare state does not merely reduce the concrete incentives that some Danes have for taking a job or to work extra in the job that one already holds. Much evidence suggests that the welfare state also has a very costly and long-lasting effect on the working ethic of Danes' (Hunnerup Dahl 2013: 2 (translated from Danish); see also the *New York Times* 2013).

Sick of work

A number of attitude studies in Sweden conclude that a significant portion of the population has come to consider that it is acceptable to live on sickness benefits without being sick. A survey from 2001, for example, showed that 41

---

3   So, even after its proposed reform package, the Danish government realises that much more needs to be done in order to encourage work.

per cent of Swedish employees believed that it was acceptable for those who were not sick but who felt stress at work to claim sickness benefit. Additionally, 44 and 48 per cent respectively believed that it was acceptable to claim sickness benefits if they were dissatisfied with their working environment or had problems within their family (Modig and Broberg 2002).

Other studies have pointed to increases in sickness absence due to sporting events. For instance, absence due to sickness increased by almost 7 per cent among men at the time of the Winter Olympics in 1988, and by 16 per cent in connection with TV broadcasts of the World Championship in cross-country skiing in 1987 (Skogman Thoursie 2004). During the 2002 football World Cup the increase in sickness absence among men was an astonishing 41 per cent. The stark difference between the events during the end of the 1980s and the beginning of the 2000s might be seen as an indication of the deterioration of work ethics over time – though all three figures are remarkably high (Persson 2005).[4]

The persistence of moral norms

This deterioration in personal responsibility and ethics supports Swedish scholar Assar Lindbeck's theory on the self-destructive dynamics of welfare states. According to this theory, changes in work ethic are related to a rising

---

4   In both cases, the sickness rate among women is used as a control for other variations.

dependence on welfare state institutions (Lindbeck 1995, 2008). Lindbeck has noted that the evidence of explicit benefit fraud in Sweden, where, for example – some individuals receive unemployment benefits or sick pay while working in the shadow economy – leads to a weakening of norms against overusing various benefit systems. Reforms to limit fraud are instrumental in order to maintain the welfare system (Lindbeck 2008).[5]

Indeed, reforms directed towards creating stronger gate-keeping functions in welfare services, in order to limit overuse, have been implemented in the Swedish welfare system, particularly during the period 2006 to 2010. Some reductions in benefit generosity have also been introduced. Interestingly, a recent paper suggests that the reforms may need to be quite far-reaching to reverse the long-term effect that the welfare state has had. Economist Martin Ljunge suggests that politicians who wish to increase the generosity of the welfare state must take into account the long-term costs of such policies (Ljunge 2013). The abstract reads (ibid. (translated from Swedish): 56):

> Younger generations use sickness insurance more often than older generations. Amongst the younger generation twenty percentage points more take a sick leave day compared with those born twenty years before, after

---

5   It is worth noting that Scandinavian countries have relatively large shadow economies compared with countries such as the US. Scandinavian shadow economies have reduced as a share of total GDP in recent years, coinciding with a shift towards greater economic freedom: see Schneider and Williams (2013) for estimations of the size of shadow economies.

other circumstances have been adjusted for. The higher demand for sick leave pay among the younger generations can be seen as a measure of how rapidly the welfare state affects attitudes towards the use of public benefits. The results have implications for economic policy. The demand for social insurance increases, even if the rules do not become more generous. Policy evaluations based on behavioural changes shortly before and after a reform can strongly under-estimate the long-term changes that are relevant for the financial integrity of a welfare state.

A recent research paper shows how welfare regimes create long-lasting dependency by looking at a natural experiment in Norway. The authors write that some claim that 'a culture has developed in which welfare use reinforces itself through the family, because parents on welfare provide information about the programme to their children, reduce the stigma of participation, or invest less in child development.' This claim is difficult to test empirically because many factors can explain the link between children's behaviour and parents' tendency to rely on welfare. However, the authors of the paper found a natural experiment that makes it possible to isolate the effect of welfare generosity (Dahl et al. 2013, quoted from abstract).

In the Norwegian welfare system, judges are sometimes appointed to look at disability insurance claims that have initially been denied. Some appeal judges are systematically more lenient when it comes to granting benefits. From the perspective of claimants, being appointed a strict or lenient judge is a random event. The researchers can therefore compare those who are granted disability insurance by a lenient judge with those who are denied the benefit by a strict judge. The conclusion is clear. The authors find 'strong evidence that welfare use in one generation causes welfare use in the next generation: when a parent is allowed DI [disability insurance] because of a lenient judge, their adult child's participation over the next five years increases by 6 percentage points. This effect grows over time, rising to 12 percentage points after ten years' (ibid., quoted from abstract).

Although Scandinavian societies have long been known for a strong work ethic and emphasis on responsibility, this has not been resistant to high taxes and the perpetuation of generous welfare programmes. Norms do have a strong persistence, as they are passed down from parents to children. But, in the long run, they adapt to changing circumstances. In the same manner that Scandinavians over a long time developed a strong work ethic and high levels of trust, they have during recent decades begun to adapt their behaviour and attitudes to generous welfare systems. This changing behaviour in part explains the political pressure to reform welfare systems in the Nordic nations.

10 NORWAY VS SWEDEN – A NATURAL EXPERIMENT IN WELFARE STATE REFORM

[T]he Norwegians are really the last Soviet-State

> Björn Rosengren, Swedish social democratic
> Minister of Enterprise in 1999, commenting to
> a journalist when he was not aware that the camera
> was running, quoted by *Svenska Dagbladet* (2011)

Sweden and Norway are, in many ways, quite comparable countries. They have a similar geographical situation, closely related cultures and similar languages. Until recently they also had similar policies. The difference is that Norway has great oil wealth and this has meant that Norway has not reformed its welfare state. Norway still has welfare systems that are so generous that the incentives for work are sometimes small or even non-existent. In a sense, a comparison of Sweden and Norway is almost a natural experiment that illuminates the consequences of welfare reform.

The centre-right government in Sweden which was in power between 2006 and 2014 focused on a broad reform agenda. The policies that were introduced included the following measures: somewhat less generous benefits;

tax reductions aimed particularly at those with lower incomes; liberalisation of temporary employment contracts; and a gate-keeping mechanism for receiving sickness and disability benefits. These policies were intended to address high hidden unemployment. Indeed, the number on sick leave and in early retirement has fallen following the reforms. In 2006, 20 per cent of the working-age population in Sweden was supported by some form of government benefit. During the following six years, the Swedish economy was significantly affected by the global financial crisis. Despite this, the share supported by government benefits fell to 14 per cent in 2012 (Statistics Sweden 2013a).[1]

In Norway the share of the population depending on public benefits was also 20 per cent in 2006. In 2012 it had been reduced by less than 1 per cent (*Aftenposten* 2013a).[2] Since Norway relies on oil wealth, the country should, if anything, have been better at creating employment following the crisis (especially given the rising oil price). That Sweden managed to reduce public benefit dependency considerably more indicates that the reforms were indeed successful.

Norway is unusual among western European countries. During recent years, almost all nations in this region have seen a dramatic fall in support for the traditional social democratic parties, which have dominated the political landscapes. The social democratic parties have adapted by

---

1   This figure is given as full-year equivalents, which means that two individuals who were on sick leave half the year each count as one individual living on benefits rather than work during that year.

2   This figure is also given as full-year equivalents.

moving towards greater emphasis on the benefits of free markets and individual responsibility. In several countries the former communist parties now claim that they fill the role of traditional social democrats. However, although Norwegian social democrats in 2013 lost an election to the centre right, the country has yet to experience a similar transition.

One consequence of the generous welfare policies in Norway is a deterioration in the work ethic. The TV series *Lilyhammer*, starring Sopranos actor Steven Van Zandt as a US expat to Norway, regularly makes fun of the lack of work discipline in the country. This phenomenon is also apparent outside popular culture. In 2014 the *Financial Times* reported: 'Norway's statistics office says many people have started to call Friday "fridag" – "free day" in Norwegian. The state railway company says commuter trains serving the capital are less full on Fridays, and the main toll road operator says traffic is noticeably quieter on Fridays and on Mondays.'

In particular, young Norwegians are adapting to a system with limited incentives for hard work. Employers are therefore turning to foreign labour, including from Sweden. Between 1990 and 2010 the number of young Swedes employed in Norway increased more than 20-fold. Swedish youth have come to make up almost one-fifth of the Norwegian capital Oslo's youth population (*Aftenposten* 2013b). One reason why Swedes are attracted to the Norwegian labour market is that wages are higher there as a result of the wealth that comes with oil revenues. Another is that the work ethic has deteriorated more in the generous

Norwegian welfare system than in the Swedish, somewhat more workfare-oriented, model.

In a recent survey three out of four Norwegian employers answered that Swedish youth working in the country have a better work ethic than Norwegian youth. Out of those questioned, 28 per cent said that Swedes between the ages of 16 and 24 years have a high work capacity. Merely 2 per cent held the same opinion for young Norwegians. The differences existed in various sectors, including both government and private employers. Stein André Haugerund, the president of the employment company Proffice which carried out the survey, argued that policy differences could explain the situation. According to Haugerund, the Norwegian welfare model has created a situation where incentives for hard work are limited, which in turn affects the behaviour of youth (*Dagens Möjligheter* 2012).

The comparison between Norway and Sweden shows that welfare reforms can play an important role in reducing exclusion from the labour market, and also in strengthening working norms. An interesting question is how sustainable the Norwegian welfare model is. The country can certainly afford its welfare system due to its oil wealth. For the same reason Norway can continue to have less economic liberty than the other Nordic nations. However, Norwegian policy makers have good reasons to be concerned about the social and economic consequences that follow long-term welfare dependency and a deterioration in the work ethic. It is also vital for the country to promote entrepreneurship and reduce state involvement in the economy rather than rely on old economic structures.

The traditional welfare state in Norway needs reforming, but the absence of fiscal constraints has limited the pressure for change. Much like the oil-rich states in the Middle East, a natural resource that should be an economic blessing has reduced political responsibility. It remains to be seen if the new centre-right government is willing to change direction. Otherwise Norway may continue to provide a contrast to the other Nordic nations, which have already reformed and increased their levels of economic liberty.[3]

---

3   As shown later, Norway has also increased the level of economic freedom over time, but less so than the other Nordic nations.

11 THE WELFARE STATE AND THE FAILURE OF IMMIGRATION POLICY

Three of the four Somali women do not work, one in three are divorced and half have more than three children.

Somali-Norwegian Kadra Yosuf (2010)
on how the generous Norwegian welfare state
paradoxically destroys family structures

Scandinavian countries are successful in many ways, both economically and socially. However, this success is not immediately translated to migrants. In fact, the Scandinavian countries have much higher unemployment rates among foreign-born residents than among natives (Table 12); the ability to integrate foreign-born residents is considerably lower than in the more market-oriented Anglo-Saxon nations.

As Danish researchers Kræn Blume and Mette Verner write, several possible theories can explain the situation. One is the 'welfare magnet hypothesis', according to which groups with low market earning potential will be drawn to countries with a high standard of living and generous systems of public transfers (Blume and Verner 2007). Indeed, economic research shows that highly qualified migrants

Table 12   Total unemployment among natives and foreign-born (percentage)

	Native born 2009	Foreign born 2009	Difference
Spain	16.0	27.4	11.4
Belgium	6.6	16.2	9.6
Finland	8.1	16.3	8.2
Sweden	7.2	15.4	8.2
France	8.8	15.1	6.3
Germany	6.8	13.0	6.1
Norway	2.6	8.4	5.9
Austria	3.9	9.5	5.6
Netherlands	3.3	8.1	4.9
Denmark	5.7	10.2	4.5
Ireland	11.2	15.4	4.3
Luxembourg	3.3	7.3	4.0
Switzerland	3.1	6.9	3.8
Iceland	7.5	11.0	3.5
Portugal	9.7	13.1	3.4
Czech Republic	6.7	9.6	2.9
Greece	9.3	12.0	2.7
Turkey	12.8	15.1	2.4
Canada	7.9	10.2	2.3
Slovenia	5.9	7.4	1.5
Australia	5.3	6.7	1.3
Estonia	14.0	14.8	0.8
United Kingdom	7.6	8.4	0.8
United States	9.4	9.4	0.0
Hungary	10.1	9.1	−1.0

Source: OECD (2011) and own calculations.

tend to be attracted to countries with low taxes and high wages for well-qualified labour. Countries with generous welfare systems and high taxes on the other hand attract immigrants with lower qualifications (Cohen and Razin 2008; Razin and Wahba 2011).

The European Commission has calculated the share of employed third-country nationals who work in high-skill occupations. Data are given for two Nordic nations, namely Finland and Sweden. In Finland, foreign-born individuals in high-skilled jobs constituted merely 0.7 per cent of the total employed population in 2012. This is one-third of the EU average and one-sixth of the UK level of 4.5 per cent. The low rate can be explained by the fact that Finland, unlike the other three Scandinavian countries, has a relatively small immigrant population (European Commission 2013).

Sweden, on the other hand, has during recent decades received high levels of immigration. In recent years the country has, in addition to refugee and family immigration, opened up its previously very strict system of labour migration, introducing perhaps the most liberal labour migration laws among the OECD. Nevertheless, only 1.6 per cent of those employed in Sweden are foreign-born individuals in high-skilled occupations (ibid.).

One explanation is that Sweden, due to high taxes and low wages for well-qualified people, is not attractive enough for talented migrants. In addition, the Swedish labour market is not well adapted for the integration of foreign-born individuals. Among those who come as refugees and as family immigrants, some have high levels of education and skills, and good labour market experience. Even this group, however, struggles to enter the labour market. Many who become employed find work well below their skill levels. This has not always been the case. During the free-market era in the first half of the 20th century, Swedish society was very successful when it came to offering foreign-born individuals good prospects in the labour market.

In 1950, the rate of employment for foreign-born residents was 20 per cent higher than that for the average citizen. By 2000, however, the rate of employment was 30 per cent lower for the foreign-born residents. Another comparison shows that, in 1968, foreign-born individuals had 22 per cent higher income from work compared with those born in Sweden. In 1999, the average income of foreign-born residents was 45 per cent lower than that of those born in Sweden (Ekberg and Hammarstedt 2002).

While racism decreased as time passed, the situation of the foreign born in the labour market worsened dramatically. A government study showed that, as late as 1978, foreign-born residents from outside the Nordic nations had a rate of employment that was only 7 per cent lower than that of native Swedes. In 1995, the gap had expanded to 52 per cent (Ekberg 1997).

Why did this drastic change occur? One reason is that immigration to Sweden moved towards refugee migration with relatively fewer economic migrants. However, the nations from which labour immigrants came to Sweden after World War II – such as Greece and Turkey – were relatively impoverished at the time. Also, many of the refugees who have come to Sweden from countries such as Chile, Iran and Iraq have been part of the educated higher and middle classes, seeking a better life abroad.

To give an illustrative example, a privileged group of well-educated Iraqi citizens fled from Saddam Hussein's Iraq to Sweden at the end of the 1980s and beginning of the 1990s. Those Iraqis who stayed in Sweden between 1987 and 1991 were 2.3 times as likely to have a higher education of more than three years compared with native Swedes. So, how well did this highly educated group do in the Swedish labour market? In 1995, only 13 per cent of the women and 23 per cent of the men from the group were employed (Rooth 1999).

Another Swedish study has calculated the incomes of immigrants to Sweden from Iran and Turkey. Between 1993 and 2000, the income from work for the average Iranian immigrant was only 61 per cent, and for the average Turkish immigrant 74 per cent, of the average income of a native Swede (Statistics Sweden and Arbetslivsinstitutet 2002). This can be contrasted with the US experience. According to the US Census for 2000, those born in Iran had an income that was 136 per cent of the average for native-born US residents. Those born in Turkey had an income of 114 per cent of the average for native-born residents (US Census 2000). Differences do exist between the individuals who migrated from Turkey and Iran to the US and those who migrated to Sweden. But these differences alone cannot explain the huge gap in outcomes. After all, many of those who left for Sweden had belonged to the Turkish or Iranian middle classes.

Outcomes for poorly educated immigrants

In 2004, when the Swedish economy was performing strongly, the employment rate among immigrants from non-Western nations in Sweden was only 48 per cent (Sanandaji 2009). It should be noted that employment in Swedish statistics also includes some people that do not hold a regular occupation, such as those participating in government-financed labour market programmes. Dependence on government welfare was nine times as high for non-Western immigrants compared with people born in Sweden the same year (Statistics Sweden 2004).

Sweden has thus gone from being a nation which successfully integrated the foreign born into the labour market, to one where many immigrants are trapped in long-term dependency on benefit payments. This change is linked to immigration policy, but also to the general economic policy. The expansion of the welfare state since the mid twentieth century has created a situation where the incentive to work has been reduced, while the incentive to live off benefit payments has increased. At the same time, regulations and trade union domination of the labour market impede entry into the workforce. As a consequence, the ability to integrate foreign-born people has significantly worsened (Sanandaji 2009).

Table 13 shows the unemployment rates of immigrants with low education levels compared with native-born individuals. In the Anglo-Saxon countries, immigrants with low education levels have, in fact, the same or lower rates of unemployment compared with natives with similar

Table 13   Unemployment among immigrants in Scandinavian and Anglo-Saxon countries (percentage of labour force in age range 15–64)

	Unemployment rate of low-educated foreign-born population	Difference between unemployment rate of low-educated foreign born and natives	Unemployment rate of highly educated foreign-born population	Difference between unemployment rate of highly educated foreign born and natives
US	14.7	–8.9	6.4	1.4
New Zealand	14.9	–2.3	5.8	1.9
Australia	10.1	–1.0	5.0	2.5
UK	8.6	–0.8	6.4	2.7
Norway	13.2	6.9	4.3	2.8
Canada	16.7	0.3	8.5	3.8
OECD average	16.9	2.7	8.4	4.0
Denmark	15.9	6.2	9.4	5.5
Sweden	26.8	10.3	11.2	8.1
Finland	23.9	8.5	12.4	8.4

Source: OECD (2012b).

educational backgrounds. In the US the unemployment level is almost 9 percentage points lower for foreign-born compared with natives among those with low education levels. This compares with a rate over 10 percentage points higher in Sweden. In Scandinavian labour markets, even immigrants with high qualifications can struggle to find suitable employment. Highly educated immigrants in Finland and Sweden have an unemployment rate over 8 percentage points higher than native-born Finns and Swedes of similar educational background. In the Anglo-Saxon countries, the difference ranges from 1.4 percentage points in the US to 2.7 percentage points in the UK.

It is interesting that Denmark, with more liberal labour market policies, has lower foreign-born unemployment than Sweden and Finland. At the same time, the Danish welfare state is not nearly as effective as the UK model in creating opportunities for immigrants. Denmark has relatively high effective minimum wages as well as generous benefits. This makes it difficult, and not always lucrative, for immigrants to get a foothold in the labour market (Brücker et al. 2012). Danish researcher Peter Nannestad (2004: 6) writes:

> In addition to broad coverage, transfer payments in the Danish welfare state are also quite generous relative to minimum wages in the labour market. Thus the welfare state weakens economic incentives for labour market participation, especially for low-skilled, low-paid, individuals. [...] the welfare state may also weaken immigrants' incentives to invest in acquiring the necessary preconditions for labour market participation, like minimum levels of language and social skills.

In Norway, much unemployment is hidden in early retirement statistics, among native-born Norwegians in general and among immigrants. One study looks at the individuals aged 30–55 who were granted a disability pension at some point between 1992 and 2003. This group includes 11 per cent of men and 16 per cent of women with a Norwegian background. Among immigrants from the

Middle East and North Africa, the figures were even higher: 25 per cent among the men and 24 per cent among the women. The authors calculate that: 'Age-adjusted relative risk of receiving a disability pension was more than three times higher for Middle Eastern/North African males that for ethnic Norwegians' (Claussen et al. 2012: 260). The fact that a significant share of Norwegians of working age at some point are granted disability pensions, often temporarily of course, strengthens the case that the system to a large degree is used as hidden unemployment.

There is no doubt that a generous welfare system initially helps many immigrant families, cushioning the transition to a new country. However, as long-term dependency grows, it can easily lead to marginalisation. The result is lasting social poverty, as welfare dependency is passed on from parents to children, in neighbourhoods where many adults do not work.

Migration, social exclusion and reactionary political forces

The failure to integrate migrants in Nordic societies is often discussed in terms of social exclusion. It is argued that those who are excluded from the labour market then do not partake in wider society. Hence, it becomes difficult to build up social capital. The skills that the immigrants come with from their countries of origin often depreciate over periods of inactivity; thus the problem perpetuates. In addition, a lack of integration breeds cultural divides that tend to lead to a decline of society-wide trust. A wide range of social challenges, including the rise of racist sentiments, follows.

Anti-immigration parties have had considerable success in Scandinavian countries recently. One example is the Danish People's Party. The party gathered over 12 per cent of the parliamentary votes during the elections of 2001, 2005, 2007 and 2011. The Danish People's Party supported a centre-right government from 2001 until 2011, when a centre-left government came to power. In Norway the Progress Party gathered 22 per cent of the votes in 2005 and 23 per cent in 2009. In 2013 the party shrank to 16 per cent. An explanation for this decline might be the killings committed by anti-immigration extremist Anders Breivik.[1] Although the Progress Party has different views from Breivik, public support for the party fell after the massacre.

Finland has historically received few refugee immigrants. The integration failures of the other Scandinavian countries might explain the rise of the anti-immigration Finns Party, previously known as the True Finns. The party went from receiving below 2 per cent of the vote in 2003 to 4 per cent in 2007. In 2011 it gained 19 per cent of the vote. Sweden continues to have a uniquely free approach to immigration. The country combines high levels of refugee and family immigrants with a welfare system that hinders integration. The result is a growing popular discontent. The Swedish anti-immigration party, the Swedish

---

1 In 2011 Breivik bombed a government building in Oslo, killing eight people. He continued by killing a further 69 individuals, mainly teenagers belonging to the youth faction of the Social Democratic Party.

Democrats, has neo-Nazi origins. Still, the party has more than doubled its support in the last four consecutive elections. The Swedish Democrats have gone from gathering 0.4 per cent of the vote in 1998 to becoming the third largest party with 13 per cent in 2014.

A discussion of immigration policy is beyond the scope of this book. Integration of foreign-born individuals is not easy in any modern economy. Even Anglo-Saxon countries face challenges relating to immigration and integration. It is, however, quite clear that Scandinavian countries experience more difficulties compared with countries with flexible labour markets and less extensive welfare systems. It is also evident that the Nordic model was more open to integration in the free-market era than after the transition to large welfare states. Sadly, the combination of inflexible labour markets and welfare entrapment limits opportunities for immigrants to climb the social ladder. This has fuelled a shift in attitudes towards immigration which is continuing to change the Nordic political landscape.

12 WELFARE STATES AND THE SUCCESS OF WOMEN

Public sector dominance of welfare sectors can be assumed to have constituted an obstacle for women's businesses.

Elisabeth Sundin and Malin Tillmar (2008: 12)

Scandinavian culture of equality

Scandinavian countries have for a long time been, and continue to be, pioneers when it comes to gender equality. Women entered the labour market early and have succeeded on their own merits to reach high political positions. However, Scandinavian countries are not necessarily leading the way if we look at the share of women who reach the top in the private sector. Welfare services monopolies, high tax wedges and social insurance systems limit women's career opportunities and enterprise.

The emergence of a large public sector has historically played an important role for women's entry into the labour market. One reason is that many women have found jobs in the public sector; another is that public services such

Figure 11 Employment rate of women aged 20–64 across the European Union (per cent)

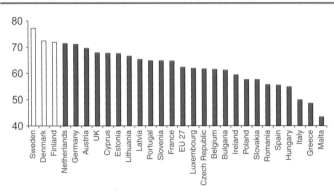

Data given for 2011. Source: Statistics Sweden (2013b).

as childcare facilitate the combination of work and the fulfilment of family responsibilities. The expansion of the public sector, not least that of childcare, in part explains why the Nordic EU members reached a high employment rate among women earlier than other Western countries, which still pertains today (Figure 11). In the long run, however, women's career success has been hampered by the fact that the labour market entry of women has been so intimately connected with the growth of the public sector.

We would expect to find many more women in top positions in the egalitarian Nordic nations. And indeed we do: at least when it comes to politics, the public sector and company boards. Often the analysis stops here, but representation on boards is, in fact, a poor measure of women's progress in the private sector.

Gender equality where it matters?

Some boards in Nordic nations are actively engaged in how the companies they represent are run. Others have a more supervisory nature, meeting a few times a year to oversee the work of the management. The select few individuals who occupy board positions – many of whom reach this position after careers in politics, academia and other non-business sectors – have prestigious jobs. They are, however, not representative of those taking the main decisions in the business sector. The important decisions are instead taken by executives and directors. Typically individuals only reach a high managerial position in the private sector after having worked for a long time in that sector or successfully started or expanded a firm as an entrepreneur. The share of women to reach executive and director positions is the best proxy for women's success in the business world.

Eurostat has gathered data for the share of women among 'directors and chief executives' in various European countries between 2008 and 2010. The data show that Nordic nations all have low levels of women at the top of businesses. In Denmark and Sweden, only one out of ten directors and chief executives in the business world are women. Finland and the UK fare slightly better. Those Central and Eastern European countries for which data exist have much higher representation.

A map of Europe (Figure 12) shows that on average, in Central and Eastern European countries, 32 per cent of directors and chief executives are women. This can be

Figure 12 Share of women among directors and chief executives

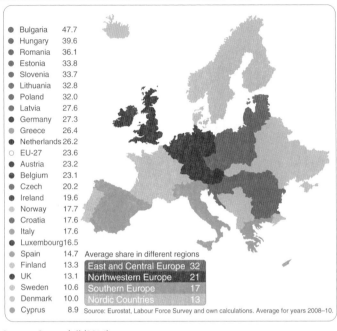

Bulgaria	47.7	
Hungary	39.6	
Romania	36.1	
Estonia	33.8	
Slovenia	33.7	
Lithuania	32.8	
Poland	32.0	
Latvia	27.6	
Germany	27.3	
Greece	26.4	
Netherlands	26.2	
EU-27	23.6	
Austria	23.2	
Belgium	23.1	
Czech	20.2	
Ireland	19.6	
Norway	17.7	
Croatia	17.6	
Italy	17.6	
Luxembourg	16.5	
Spain	14.7	
Finland	13.3	
UK	13.1	
Sweden	10.6	
Denmark	10.0	
Cyprus	8.9	

Average share in different regions

Region	
East and Central Europe	32
Northwestern Europe	21
Southern Europe	17
Nordic Countries	13

Source: Eurostat, Labour Force Survey and own calculations. Average for years 2008–10.

Source: Sanandaji (2014).

compared with 21 per cent in Northwestern European countries, 17 per cent in Southern European countries and just 13 per cent in the Nordic nations. Bulgaria, with female work participation levels lower than the EU average, has almost half of the director and chief executive positions filled by women (Sanandaji 2014). Other measures support this analysis. For example, based on interviews with 6,500 companies around the world, the firm Grant Thornton estimates that around four out of ten managers in the three Baltic nations are female, compared with around a quarter in the Nordic nations (Grant Thornton 2013).

Economists Magnus Henrekson and Mikael Stenkula have written a scientific review entitled 'Why are there so few female top executives in egalitarian welfare states?' Through a comparison of Anglo-Saxon and Northern European countries, the authors show that the Nordic nations are indeed 'gender equal' in many ways, but they have lower representation of women in top positions than in Anglo-Saxon societies (Henrekson and Stenkula 2009).

Indeed, these problems have been noted for some years. In 1998 the International Labor Office published a report entitled 'Gender and Jobs: Sex Segregation of Occupations in the World'. There it was noted that an unusually gender-segregated labour market had developed in Scandinavian countries, since many women worked in the public rather than the private sector. The report concluded: 'in terms of differences amongst industrialized countries, several studies comment on how Nordic countries, and in particular Sweden, have among the greatest inequalities' (Anker 1998: 48).

The overall picture is thus clear: few women in the Nordic nations reach the position of business leaders, and even fewer manage to climb to the very top positions of directors and chief executives. How can egalitarian Scandinavian countries, in most regards world leaders in gender equality, have low rates of female directors and chief executives, while the nations of Central and Eastern Europe are leaders in terms of women in senior positions?

Inequality in Scandinavia and the nature of the welfare state

A key explanation lies in the nature of the welfare state. In Scandinavia, female-dominated sectors such as health care and education are mainly run by the public sector. A study from the Nordic Innovation Centre (2007: 12–13) concludes:

> Nearly 50 per cent of all women employees in Denmark are employed in the public sector. Compared to the male counterpart where just above 15 per cent are employed in the public sector. This difference alone can explain some of the gender gap with respect to entrepreneurship. The same story is prevalent in Sweden.

The lack of competition reduces long-term productivity growth and overall levels of pay in the female-dominated public sector. It also combines with union wage setting to create a situation where individual hard work is not rewarded significantly: wages are flat and wage rises follow seniority, according to labour union contracts, rather than individual achievement. Women in Scandinavia can of course become managers within the public sector, but the opportunities for individual career paths, and certainly for entrepreneurship, are typically more limited compared with in the private sector.

The former planned economies in Central and Eastern Europe are well behind in terms of attitudes towards gender equality. However, during recent years many of these nations have transitioned to market economies which are often more free than the Scandinavian countries, not least when it comes to the issue of welfare monopolies. In these countries, the work patterns of women tend to be more similar to those of men than in Scandinavia. The average employed man in the Nordics works between 16 per cent (Finland) and 27 per cent (Norway) hours more than the average woman. In Lithuania the gap is 13 per cent, and in Latvia and Estonia merely 7 per cent. Bulgaria is unique as the only European Union nation where women actually work more (1 per cent more) hours than men (Statistics Sweden 2012, own calculations).

Liberalisation and opportunities for women

Since the beginning of the 1990s, liberalisation has begun to open up opportunities for women's entrepreneurship in the Nordics. Even the Swedish welfare system has increasingly opened up to private firms. This has given a particular boost to women's self-employment. For example, among the new firms that were formed in education during 2009 and 2010, 50 per cent were run by women. An additional 6 per cent had both women and men in executive positions. Among the firms formed in health and caring services during the same period, 58 per cent were run by women. A further 11 per cent had both men and women in executive positions. The public sector still remains dominant in welfare provision. Therefore only 7 per cent of newly formed businesses in Sweden were founded within the health, caring and education sectors. However, 11 per cent of companies headed by at least one woman were founded in these sectors. In addition, 15 per cent of the total new employment opportunities for women were created in these sectors (Sanandaji 2013).

An important lesson is that private competition in welfare services can boost business ownership and private sector job growth among women. This, in turn, can provide alternative career opportunities for those who would otherwise be confined to public sector monopolies. While the Scandinavian countries are uniquely gender equal in many respects, their political structures hinder women's career success and entrepreneurship.

13 ROCK STARS OF FREE-MARKET RECOVERY

Where tax goes up to 60 per cent, and everybody's happy
paying it

> Headline describing Sweden in *The Observer* (2008),
> printed during a time when far-reaching tax
> reductions were taking place in the country

Where do we find the nations with the highest tax levels?
In the mid 1990s the answer was quite clear: we find them
in Western Europe, and particularly in the Nordics. In 1996
both Denmark and Sweden had a tax take of 49 per cent of
GDP, followed closely by Finland with 47 per cent. Thanks
to its oil wealth, Norway could afford a Nordic welfare
model with taxes at 41 per cent of GDP. And where do we
find the high-tax nations today? Looking at tax data from
2012, the answer is again among the Western European
welfare states. However, tax regimes in this part of the
world have now converged. As shown in Table 14, Sweden
and Finland have reduced their tax burdens significantly
over the period. A smaller shift is evident in Denmark. Norway, which had a lower tax rate to begin with, has increased
it, as have some other Western European countries. Today

Table 14   Tax take (per cent of GDP)

	1996	2006	2012	Change 1996–2012
Sweden	49.4	48.1	44.3	−5.1
Finland	47.1	43.5	44.1	−3.0
Netherlands	40.9	39.1	38.6*	−2.4
Denmark	49.2	49.0	48.0	−1.2
Austria	42.8	43.0	43.2	0.4
France	44.2	43.6	45.3	1.1
Norway	40.9	43.1	42.2	1.4
Belgium	43.9	44.4	45.3	1.4
Italy	41.6	40.8	44.4	2.8

* Data given for 2011.
Source: OECD Stat Extract and own calculations.

France and Belgium have surpassed the tax burden of all Scandinavian countries.

The shifting sands of economic freedom

Of course, taxes are far from the only indicator of economic policy. A range of other factors, such as trade openness, policy towards business and the protection of property rights, affect the opportunities for job creation, competition and growth. The Index of Economic Freedom, published by the Heritage Foundation in partnership with the *Wall Street Journal*, ranks countries based on a broad set of indicators of economic freedom. The Western European welfare states can, overall, be said to combine large public

Table 15   Heritage/WSJ economic freedom score

	1996	2006	2015	Change 1996–2015
Sweden	61.8	70.9	72.7	10.9
Finland	63.7	72.9	73.4	9.7
Denmark	67.3	75.4	76.3	9.0
Norway	65.4	67.9	71.8	6.4
Netherlands	69.7	75.4	73.7	4.0
Belgium	66.0	71.8	68.8	2.8
Austria	68.9	71.1	71.2	2.3
Italy	60.8	62.0	61.7	0.9
France	63.7	61.1	62.5	−1.2

Source: Heritage Foundation and *Wall Street Journal*, Economic Freedom Index and own calculations.

sectors and high taxation with relatively free economic policies. But the differences between them are significant, and the direction of change has varied considerably during the last two decades.

When the index of economic freedom was first published in the mid-1990s, it showed that the Netherlands and Austria were the most market liberal of the nine Western European countries listed in Table 15. Sweden and Italy were at the bottom. Since then economic freedom has risen in most of Western Europe, particularly in the four Nordic economies. In the 2015 edition of the index, Denmark had become the 11th freest economy in the world, ranking higher than both the US and the UK. Finland and Sweden reached 19th and 23rd positions respectively. Norway, slower to reform, ranked in 27th position, one place below Iceland. All the Nordic countries now have higher levels of economic freedom than Austria (30th), Belgium (40th), France (73rd) and Italy (80th) (Heritage Foundation and *Wall Street Journal* 2015).

So, while Nordic nations have converged towards countries such as France, Belgium and Austria in terms of the level of taxation – they have far outpaced them in overall economic freedom. The shift in economic policy is significant. If Sweden had retained its 1996 economic freedom score, it would be the 78th freest economy today, with a lower score than Saudi Arabia and Samoa. If Finland had not reformed, it would today be the 68th freest economy, one position below Panama. Only Denmark would do reasonably well, at 49, just below Spain.

An alternative to the Economic Freedom Index is the Economic Freedom of the World index published by the Canadian Fraser Institute (2014). This index measures five dimensions of economic freedom: size of government; legal structure and security of property rights; access to sound money; freedom to exchange with foreigners; and the regulation of credit, labour and business. Andreas Bergh and Magnus Henrekson have found that, between 1970 and 2004, Sweden and other Scandinavian nations scored poorly on the size of government. However, on the other four dimensions, the Scandinavian nations had reached higher scores than other groups of industrialised nations. The two economists conclude that Scandinavian countries have compensated for a large public sector by increasing economic liberty in other areas (Bergh and Henrekson 2010).

Figure 13 Heritage/WSJ Economic Freedom Index – average overall score

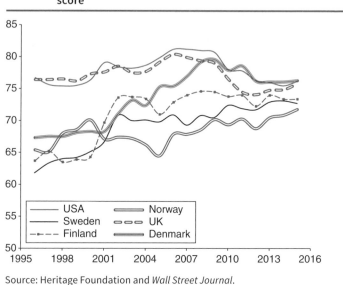

Source: Heritage Foundation and *Wall Street Journal*.

Both indices reinforce the notion that the Nordic nations are tentatively returning to their free-market roots. In Figure 13, the trend of scores in the Heritage and *Wall Street Journal* index is shown. Much of the gap in economic freedom that existed between the Nordic nations and the US and the UK has today disappeared – since the Nordics have increased economic freedom while the two Anglo-Saxon countries have moved in the opposite direction. Scandinavian countries are no longer outliers.

As shown in Table 16, Scandinavian countries score highly on protection of property rights, freedom from corruption, business freedom, investment freedom, monetary

Table 16 Economic freedom score in 2015 and changes from 1996 to 2015

			Score in 2015		
	Property rights	Freedom from corruption	Business freedom	Investment freedom	Financial freedom
Denmark	95.0	91.0	97.4	90.0	80.0
Sweden	90.0	89.0	87.9	90.0	80.0
Finland	90.0	89.0	92.6	90.0	80.0
Norway	90.0	86.0	92.1	75.0	60.0
			Change since 1996		
	Property rights	Freedom from corruption	Business freedom	Investment freedom	Financial freedom
Denmark	5.0	1.0	12.4	20.0	10.0
Sweden	20.0	−1.0	17.9	20.0	30.0
Finland	0	−1.0	37.6	20.0	30.0
Norway	0	−4.0	22.1	5.0	10.0
			Score in 2015		
	Monetary Freedom	Trade Freedom	Labour freedom	Fiscal freedom	Government spending
Denmark	87.6	88.0	92.1	39.6	1.8
Sweden	85.5	88.0	54.0	43.0	19.2
Finland	79.9	88.0	54.8	66.4	3.6
Norway	81.7	89.4	48.2	52.1	43.8
			Change since 1996		
	Monetary freedom	Trade freedom	Labour freedom*	Fiscal freedom	Government spending
Denmark	−3.8	10.2	−7.8	8.1	1.8
Sweden	1.0	11.0	−11.2	−2.2	19.2
Finland	−2.4	10.2	4.9	8.0	3.6
Norway	0	20.4	−1.1	−6.7	34.9

Source: Heritage Foundation and *Wall Street Journal*.
*Data for labour freedom is not given in the index before 2005. The change thus reflects the period 2005–14.

freedom and financial freedom. The overall scores in these areas have also improved over time. These areas of economic freedom are not necessarily in conflict with a Nordic welfare state model. Even social democratic politicians in the Scandinavian countries have generally (except in the 1960s and 1970s) fostered basic freedom of enterprise.

Trade freedom has improved in Scandinavian countries from already high levels. Labour freedom has, however, reduced, though remains at high levels in Denmark and is increasing somewhat in Finland. Fiscal freedom is still low due to the high tax burdens and marginal tax rates. In the mid 1990s Denmark, Sweden and Finland all scored zero on government spending, reflecting the lowest level of freedom recorded. There have been some significant improvements in this regard. There is still substantial room for improvement in relation to government spending, fiscal freedom and labour market freedom. However, the general picture is that Scandinavia is not exceptional in the industrialised world or within Europe when it comes to economic freedom.

Varying approaches to reform

Some of the reforms in the Nordic nations have been more far-reaching than in other modern economies. One such example is Denmark's 'flexicurity' system which combines welfare safety nets with a liberal labour market. The term was first coined in the 1990s by the social democratic Prime Minister of Denmark, Poul Nyrup Rasmussen. In many respects, Sweden has led the way in school reform since the beginning of the 1990s. School vouchers have been successfully introduced, creating competition within the framework of public financing. These reforms surpass even those in the US. Similar systems are increasingly being implemented in other government programmes such as health care and elderly care. In addition, the Swedish pension system has been partly privatised, giving citizens some control over their mandated retirement savings. The state liability for future pensions is now much more effectively controlled (see, for example, Freeman et al. 2010).

Undeniably, Sweden was the more socialist of the Scandinavian countries a few decades ago. It is also the country that has reformed the most. Following a series of pro-market reforms, including significant tax cuts, Sweden showed an impressive economic performance during the crisis of 2008/2009. This prompted the *Washington Post* (2011) to refer to the nation as the 'rock star of the recovery', praising among other things Swedish fiscal conservatism.[1] Pragmatic reforms towards greater levels of economic freedom, and stronger incentives for work rather than welfare, have proven a successful path for the country. These policies stand in contrast to the failed experiment with third-way socialism for which Sweden is still famous abroad.

Denmark and Finland never experimented with socialism to the same extent. Nevertheless, both countries have reformed. Norway's oil wealth has, as discussed in the previous chapter, stood in the way of labour market and

---

1   The *Financial Times* has also praised Sweden's new economic policy, by ranking finance minister Anders Borg as the finance minister of the year (*Financial Times* 2011).

welfare reforms. But even in Norway some market reforms have been implemented and more are likely to follow.

Many still see Scandinavian countries as a bastion of socialism. But they are not – at least they are not when compared with other European countries, including the UK. The Scandinavian countries are still unique in many regards. When it comes to economic freedom and taxation, however, they are today more centrist than their reputation suggests.

14 SCANDINAVIAN UNEXCEPTIONALISM

For progressives, the Nordic countries represent a post-modern Cockaigne, in which economic egalitarianism is balanced with personal autonomy in a way that communism never achieved. For conservatives, on the other hand, 'Sweden' is shorthand for the fusion of an infantilizing welfare state with unusually suffocating political correctness.

Samuel Goldman in *The American Conservative* (2013)

Scandinavian countries are not exempt from economic laws

Many have long seen the Scandinavian countries as living proof that high taxes and generous welfare systems combine to create the optimal economic and political system. The welfare systems in Denmark, Finland, Norway and Sweden do offer various services to their citizens, not least the less well off. But these systems come at a cost. Scandinavian countries have never been an exception to the normal economic rules. These societies were successful when their states were smaller during the first half of the 20th century. Much of the social and economic progress for which the Nordics are admired happened when the countries had small or moderately sized welfare states. When the public sectors expanded in size, progress stalled. The Scandinavian countries became successful again after returning – to an extent – to their free-market roots. Despite some reforms, even today high taxes, generous welfare benefits and rigid labour market regulations hinder development – just as these features do in many other developed countries. It is true that Scandinavian countries compensate for high taxes and labour market rigidities by following liberal policies in other areas, such as business freedom and openness to trade. Again, as in other countries, this has helped ensure moderate levels of economic growth.

Culture came first

Nordic nations have long relied on a culture that generates economic success and positive social norms. Historical factors can explain why unusually high levels of trust, a strong work ethic and an emphasis on individual responsibility developed in these cold lands, inhabited for long by independent farmers not generally subject to feudal systems. It is not the welfare state that created high levels of social capital: the relationship is the other way around. In the early days, the unique culture of success in the Nordic countries meant that high taxes and welfare benefits could be introduced with limited avoidance and shirking. However, this changed over time as norms adjusted to the new economic circumstances. It takes time for deep-rooted social behaviour to adapt. As has been shown, Nordic citizens now have unusually high levels of sickness absence (despite being healthy societies), high youth unemployment and a poor record for integrating migrants into the labour force. In response to these trends, policies have been introduced to try to strengthen incentives to work, but further reforms are needed.

Simply adopting a Nordic welfare system is not the key to success. It is no coincidence that other parts of the world, such as the US, the UK and southern European nations, have been less successful in introducing welfare states. Copying Nordic policies is not the same as copying their societies and all the preconditions that allowed Nordic welfare states to work satisfactorily for a while. As has been shown, Nordic descendants in the US still today have high living standards and low poverty levels without relying on Nordic welfare states: it is culture and not welfare that has led to the outcomes social democrats admire. Indeed, Scandinavian Americans are even more prosperous than their cousins who did not migrate. A simplistic idealisation of Scandinavian social democracy fails to capture the true roots of societal features.

There are many questions that left-leaning admirers of Scandinavian systems fail to answer, because they do not examine cause and causality in more detail. Why is it, for example, that Iceland, with a moderately sized welfare sector, has outpaced the four major Scandinavian countries in terms of life expectancy and infant mortality? Why does Iceland top the income equality league? This small country certainly does not benefit from its isolated geography or harsh climate. Clearly, a bigger welfare state does not translate into better welfare within the Nordic countries. Also, why does Denmark with the largest welfare state as measured by the scope of tax revenues, fare less well than other Nordic societies? The simple explanation is that there are cultural differences relating to lifestyle. Culture and causality are important issues that admirers of the radical Swedish third-way interlude never seem to investigate.

Early Scandinavian free-market success

At heart, the success of Scandinavian countries is a free-market success story during the period before the 1970s and then in more recent years. Few other groups of countries illustrate the ability of free markets to promote the general welfare as the Nordics. During the late 19th century and the first half of the 20th century, these nations showed that free markets combined with small public sectors and low taxation could lead to wealth creation, an ability to grow out of the Great Depression through entrepreneurship and very even income distributions. It is true that, particularly in Sweden, there was experimentation with radical third-way socialism. This relatively brief experiment in the 1960s and the 1970s was a failed parenthesis in the country's history. Since then, Sweden has increased its level of economic freedom considerably, as have other Nordic nations. Even after ambitious reforms, many problems remain that are linked to the scope of the welfare regimes and state involvement. This is especially true in relation to the opportunities granted to immigrants to integrate and, outside Denmark, job creation.

The social democratic interlude, large welfare systems and social poverty

Welfare systems in Scandinavian countries have been and continue to be popular. In many ways they are also well functioning. However, their foundation is partly based on systematically hiding the scope of taxation from the citizens. It is true that welfare systems have reduced poverty. However, especially in the second generation, they have also created a form of social poverty of the same type that is apparent in the countries from which many of the admirers of the Scandinavian systems come. Detailed research clearly shows that welfare systems have formed a culture of dependency which is passed on from parents to children.

Nordic welfare works, when it is kept within bounds and combined with free markets and labour market reforms. However, generous welfare regimes, as still exist in Norway, do not produce socially desirable outcomes.

A tentative return to free markets

Since the 1980s, there has been a tentative return to free markets. In education in Sweden, parental choice has been promoted. There has also been reform to pensions systems, sickness benefits and labour market regulations, though the precise nature of reforms varies between countries. Very few wish to reverse these reforms, which have been successful in improving educational quality and labour market outcomes. Furthermore, the level of taxation and government spending in Scandinavian countries, though still high by historical and international standards, is no longer significantly higher than other EU countries. Economic freedom has increased in Scandinavia more rapidly than in most other developed countries and the relative decline of Scandinavian living standards has now been reversed.

In a sense, Paul Krugman is right: a forced walking tour of Stockholm disproves the idea of the collapsing welfare states of Europe. Such a walking tour also provides evidence that ambitious market reforms of welfare systems can prevent their stagnation. But we should not be prisoners of the present. An historical tour can teach us even more important lessons. Such a tour may especially teach Paul Krugman that Scandinavian countries have been rather unexceptional. The normal economic rules apply: incentives, economic freedom, culture and a regime of good governance all matter when it comes to economic success. The effects of policy in the three eras roughly defined by the periods 1900–60, 1960–90 and 1990 to the present, have been more or less as economists would have predicted. The question that remains is whether Scandinavian countries will continue their return to the free-market roots that have historically served them so well. If so, the Nordic culture of success can be combined with sound policies to allow growth, innovation and entrepreneurship to flourish.

REFERENCES

Abramitzky, R., Boustan, L. P. and Eriksson, K. (2012) Europe's tired, poor, huddled masses: self-selection and economic outcomes in the age of mass migration. *American Economic Review* 102(5): 1832–1856.

Aftenposten (2013a) Under deg som statsminister har antallet som står utenfor arbeidslivet økt, 19 August.

Aftenposten (2013b) Innvandring gir knallhard konkurranse om ungdomsjobbene, 7 October.

Anker, R. (1998) Gender and jobs: sex segregation of occupations in the world. International Labour Office.

Atkinson, A. B. and Søgaard, J. E. (2013) The long-run history of income inequality in Denmark: top incomes from 1870 to 2010. EPRU Working Paper Series, Department of Economics, University of Copenhagen.

Axelsson, S. (2006) Entreprenören från sekelskifte till sekelskifte – kan företag växa i Sverige? In *Svensk utvecklingskraft* (ed. D. Johansson and N. Karlsson). Stockholm: Ratio.

Baker, S. H. (1983) The determinants of median voter tax liability: an empirical test of the fiscal illusion hypothesis. *Public Finance Quarterly* 11(1): 95–108.

BBC News (2013) Australia ranked 'happiest' developed nation again, 28 May.

Beddy, J. P. (1943) A comparison of the principal economic features of Eire and Denmark. *Journal of the Statistical and Social Inquiry Society of Ireland* 1943: 189–220.

Berggren, N., Elinder, M. and Jordahl, H. (2008) Trust and growth: a shaky relationship. *Empirical Economics* 35: 251–274.

Bergh, A. and Bjørnskov, C. (2011) Historical trust levels predict the current size of the welfare state. *Kyklos* 64(1): 1–19.

Bergh, A. and Henrekson, M. (2010) *Government Size and Implications for Economic Growth*. Washington, DC: AEI Press.

Bernitz, B. K., Grees, N., Randers, M. J., Gerner, U. and Bergendorff, S. (2013) Young adults in disability benefits in 7 countries. *Scandinavian Journal of Public Health* 41(12): 3–26.

Bjuggren, C. M. and Johansson, D. (2009) Privat och offentlig sysselsättning i Sverige 1950–2005. *Ekonomisk Debatt* 1:1.

Blanchard, O. and Perotti, R. (2002) An empirical characterization of the dynamic effects of changes in government spending and taxes on output. *Quarterly Journal of Economics* 117: 1329–1368.

Brandolini, A., Smeeding, T. M. and Sierminska, E. (2008) Comparing wealth distribution across rich countries: first results from the Luxembourg wealth study. Bank of Italy Research Paper A7.

Brücker, H., Jahn, E. and Upward, R. (2012) Migration and imperfect labor markets: theory and cross-country evidence from Denmark, Germany and the UK. Norface Migration Discussion Paper 2012-20.

Blume, K. and Verner, M. (2007) Welfare dependency among Danish immigrants. *European Journal of Political Economy* 23(2): 453–471.

Buchanan, J. (1960) *Fiscal Theory and Political Economy*. Chapel Hill, NC: University of North Carolina Press.

Business Insider (2012) Bruce Springsteen wants the United States to be more like Sweden, 17 February.

Claussen, B., Smeby, L. and Bruusgaard, D. (2012) Disability pension rates among immigrants in Norway. *Journal of Immigrant and Minority Health* 14(2): 259–263.

CME (2015) Data gathered 1 February from http://www.child-mortality.org.

Cohen, A. and Razin, A. (2008) The skill composition of immigrants and the generosity of the welfare state: free vs. policy-controlled migration. NBER Working Paper 14459.

Cohen, L., Coval, J. and Malloy, C. (2011) Do powerful politicians cause corporate downsizing? NBER Working Paper 15839.

Confederation of Swedish Enterprise (2006) Utanförskap och arbetslöshet – en exkluderande arbetsmarknad!

Dagbladet (2012) En «trygdesnylters» bekjennelser, 31 March.

Dagens Industri (2006) Sverige världsmästare i 'jobless growth', 27 January.

Dagens Möjligheter (2012) Svensk arbetsmoral utklassar norrmännens, 14 November.

Dagens Nyheter (2012) The Boss vill göra Amerika lite svenskare, 17 February.

Dahl, G. B., Kostol, A. R. and Mogstad, M. (2013) Family welfare cultures. Working Paper.

Danish Employers' Confederation (1999) Danish Employers' Confederation's Labour Market Report 1999 – English Summary.

Delhy, J. and Newton, K. (2005) Predicting cross-national levels of social trust: global patterns or nordic exceptionalism? *European Sociological Review* 21: 311–327.

Economist (2012) The Nokia effect, 25 August.

Economist (2013a) What makes Nordic countries the envy of the world, 2 February.

Economist (2013b) The rich cousin, 2 February.

Edling, J. (2005) Alla behövs – Blott arbetsmarknadsåtgärder skapar inga nya jobb.

Edling, J. (2010) *Agenda för Sverige*. Stockholm: Ekerlids.

Ekberg, J. (1997) Svårt för de nya svenskarna att få jobb. Statens Invandrarverk.

Ekberg, J. and Hammarstedt, M. (2002) 20 år med allt sämre arbetsmarknadsintegration för invandrare. *Ekonomisk Debatt* 4: 343.

Ekonomifakta 2014 Privat och offentlig sysselsättning – historiskt. Data gathered 23 February from http://www.ekonomifakta .se/sv/Fakta/Arbetsmarknad/Sysselsattning/Privat-och -offentlig-sysselsattning--historiskt/.

European Commission (2013) Attracting highly qualified and qualified third-country nationals to the EU. EMN Inform.

Financial Times (2011) Moderate with a tonsorial twist, 23 November.

Financial Times (2014) Norway: cruise control, 6 February.

Fogel, R. (1999) Catching up with the economy. Speech during meeting arranged by American Economic Association in New York, 4 January.

Fraser Institute (2014) Economic Freedom of the World 2014 Annual Report.

Freeman, R. B., Swedenborg, B. and Topel, R. H. (2010) *Reforming the Welfare State: Recovery and Beyond in Sweden*. University of Chicago Press, National Bureau of Economic Research.

Fregert, K. and Pehkonen, J. (2008) Causes of structural unemployment in Finland and Sweden 1990–2004. In *The Crisis of the 1990s in Finland and Sweden. The Nordic Experience of Financial Liberalization* (ed. L. Jonung, J. Kiander and P. Vartia). Cheltenham: Edward Elgar.

Goldman, S. (2013) The Nordic mirage. *The American Conservative*, 2 April.

Grant Thornton (2013) Women in senior management: setting the stage for growth.

Hansen, M. L. (2012) Det private forbrug pr. inbygger ligger nr. 14 i OECD – En nedgang fra en 6. plads 1970. CEPOS.

Hansson, Å. (2009) Vad kostar beskattning – analys av den samhällsekonomiska kostnaden av beskattning. Confederation of Swedish Enterprise.

Heinemann, F. (2008) Is the welfare state self-destructive? A study of government benefit morale. *Kyklos* 61(2): 237–257.

Henrekson, M. (2007) Välfärdsstaten och entreprenörskapet. IFN Policy Paper 16.

Henrekson, M. and Stenkula, M. (2009) Why are there so few female top executives in egalitarian welfare states? IFN Working Paper 786.

Herin, J., Jakobsson, U. and Rydeman, A. (2006) Ge de arbetslösa en chans – 150 000 nya jobb genom halverade arbetsgivaravgifter. Den Nya Välfärden.

Heritage Foundation and *Wall Street Journal*, Index of Economic Freedom database.

Hertz, T. (2008) A group-specific measure of intergenerational persistence. *Economics Letters* 100(3): 415–417.

Holmlund, B. and Söderström, M. (2007) Estimating income responses to tax changes: a dynamic panel data approach. IZA Discussion Paper 3088.

Honkapohja, S. and Koskela, E. (1999) The economic crisis of the 1990s in Finland. *Economic Policy* 14(29): 399–436.

Honningdal Grytten, O. (2008) Why was the Great Depression not so great in the Nordic countries? Economic policy and unemployment. *Journal of European Economic History* 37(2/3): 369–393, 395–403.

Huffington Post (2014) Canada ranks fifth on OECD's Better Life Index, 5 May.

Hunnerup Dahl, C. (2013) Velfæerdsstat og arbejdsmoral. CEPOS.

Johnson, A. (2006) Tidernas entreprenörer i Sverige. Gleerups Utbildning.

Jyllands Posten (2012) Rødt angreb på velfærdsstaten, 25 March.

Kotkin, J. (2009) Is Obama separating from his Scandinavian muse? *New Geography*, 11 December.

Krantz, O. (1997) Svensk ekonomisk tillväxt under 1900-talet – en problematisk historia. *Ekonomisk Debatt* 1.

Kristensen, P. H. (1989) Denmark: an experimental laboratory for new industrial models. *Entrepreneurship and Regional Development* 1(3): 245–255.

Larsson, L. (2009) Jakten på den dolda skatten. Timbro.

Lindbeck, A. (1995) Hazardous welfare-state dynamics. *American Economic Review, Papers and Proceedings* 85(2): 9–15.

Lindbeck, A. (1997) The Swedish experiment. *Journal of Economic Literature* 35: 1273–1319.

Lindbeck, A., Nyberg, S. and Weibull, J. W. (1999) Social norms and economic incentives in the welfare state. *Quarterly Journal of Economics* 114(1): 1–35.

Lindbeck, A. (2003) An essay on welfare state dynamics. CESifo Working Paper Series 976.

Lindbeck, A. and Nyberg, S. (2006) Raising children to work hard: altruism, work norms, and social insurance. *Quarterly Journal of Economics* 121(4): 1473–1503.

Lindbeck, A. (2008) Prospects for the welfare state. Seminar Paper 755, Institute for International Economic Studies, Stockholm University.

Ljunge, M. (2013) Yngre generationers högre sjukskrivningstal – ett mått på hur snabbt välfärdsstaten förändrar normer. *Ekonomisk Debatt* 5: 56–61.

Logue, J. (1979) The welfare state: victim of its success. *Daedalus* 108(4): 69–87.

Logue, J. (1985) Will success spoil the welfare state? Solidarity and egotism in Scandinavia. *Dissent*, Winter 96-104.

Ljungqvist, L. and Sargent, T. (2006) Hur Sveriges arbetslöshet blev mer lik Europas. In *Att reformera välfärdsstaten – amerikanskt perspektiv på den svenska modellen*. NBER Report.

Lundby Hansen, M. (2011) En flad skat på 40 PCT øger arbejdsudbuddet markant. CEPOS.

Maddison, A. (1982) *Phases of Capitalist Development*. Oxford University Press.

Maddison, A. (2010) Historical statistics of the world economy: 1–2008 AD. Data file downloaded 3 December from http://www.ggdc.net/MADDISON/Historical_Statistics/horizontal-file_02-2010.xls.

McKinsey Quarterly (2006) Sweden's growth paradox, June.

Michau, J.-B. (2009) Unemployment insurance and cultural transmission: theory and application to European unemployment. CEP Discussion Paper 936, Centre for Economic Performance, London School of Economics and Political Science, London, UK.

Mitchell, D. J. (2007) What can the United States learn from the Nordic model? *Cato Institute Policy Analysis* 603, 5 November.

Modig, A. and Broberg, K. (2002) Är det OK att sjukskriva sig om man inte är sjuk? Memo T22785, TEMO, Stockholm.

Nannestad, P. (2004) Immigration as a challenge to the Danish welfare state? *European Journal of Political Economy* 20(3): 755–767.

National Public Radio (2010) Denmark thrives despite high taxes, 29 January.

Nelson, R. H. (2010) Max Weber revisited. In *Religion, Economy and Cooperation* (ed. I. Pyysiäinen). Berlin: Walter de Gruyter.

New Geography (2010) Is Sweden a false utopia?, 2 May.

New York Times (2007) High income taxes in Denmark worsen a labor shortage, 5 December.

New York Times (2010) The limits of policy, 3 May.

New York Times (2011) Socialist hellhole blogging. The conscience of a liberal, Paul Krugmans blog, 19 August: http://krugman.blogs.nytimes.com/2011/08/19/socialist-hellhole-blogging/

New York Times (2013) Danes rethink a welfare state ample to a fault, 10 April.

Nordic Innovation Centre (2007) Women Entrepreneurship – A Nordic Perspective.

Notten, G. and de Neubourg, C. (2011) Monitoring absolute and relative povety: 'Not enough' is not the same as 'much less'. *Review of Income and Wealth* 57(2): 247–269.

Observer (2008) Where tax goes up to 60 per cent, and everybody's happy paying it, 16 November.

OECD (2009) Sickness, disability and work – keeping on track in the economic downturn. Background paper presented at High-Level Forum, Stockholm, 14–15 May 2009.

OECD (2011) *OECD Factbook 2011–2012: Economic, Environmental and Social Statistics*. Paris: OECD.

OECD (2012a) *OECD Economic Surveys – Norway*. Paris: OECD.

OECD (2012b) Indicators of integration of immigrants and their children. Data taken from interactive data tool available at http://www.oecd.org/migration/integrationindicators/.

OECD (2013) *Finland – Fit for the Future.* Paris: OECD.

Ohanian, L., Raffo, A. and Rogerson, R. (2008) Long-term changes in labor supply and taxes: evidence from OECD countries, 1956–2004. *Journal of Monetary Economics* 55(8): 1353–1362.

Økonomi og indenrigsministeriet (2013) Økonomisk redegørelse, August.

O'Rourke, K. H. (2003) Property rights, social cohesion and innovation: evidence from the creameries. Mimeo, Trinity College Dublin.

O'Rourke, K. H. (2006) Late 19th century Denmark in an Irish mirror: land tenure, homogeneity and the roots of Danish success. In *The State of Denmark: Small States, Corporatism and the Varieties of Capitalism.* Montreal: McGill-Queen's University Press.

Persson, M. (2005) Korta sjukskrivningar under fotbolls-VM 2002 – en empirisk studie. Mimeo, Department of Economics, Uppsala University.

Pirttilä, J. and Selin, H. (2011) Skattepolitik och sysselsättning: Hur väl fungerar det svenska systemet? Appendix 12 to Långtidsutredningen 2011.

Politiken (2013) Corydon: Konkurrencestat er ny velfærdsstat, 23 August.

Popenoe, D. (1994) Scandinavian welfare. *Society* 31(6): 78–81.

Razin, A. and Wahba, J. (2011) Free vs. controlled migration: bilateral country study. NBER Working Paper 16831.

Ringholm, B. (2002) Därför är vi bättre på tillväxt än borgarna. In *Dagens Industri*, 16 August.

Rogerson R. (2009) Market work, home work, and taxes: a cross-country analysis. *Review of International Economics* 17(3): 588–601.

Roine, J. and Waldenström, D. (2008) The evolution of top incomes in an egalitarian society: Sweden, 1903–2004. *Journal of Public Economics* 92(1–2): 366–387.

Rooth, D.-O. (1999) Refugee immigrants in Sweden: educational investment and labor market integration. *Lund Economic Studies* 84.

Sachs, J. D. (2006) The social welfare state, beyond ideology. *Scientific American*, 16 October.

Sanandaji, N. (2009) *Mellanförskap*. Malmö: Captus.

Sanandaji, N. (2010b) Entreprenörer som går mot strömmen – Vad 90-talskrisens succé-företagare kan lära om dagens utmaningar. Fores.

Sanandaji, N. (2011) Arbetslinjen på undantag – Dold arbetslöshet och förtidspension bland unga. Timbro.

Sanandaji, N. (2013) *Att spräcka glastaken*. Stockholm: Volante.

Sanandaji, N. (2014) Female executives across the European Union. *New Geography*, 16 January.

Sanandaji, T. (2010a) Proving Bo Rothstein wrong: why do Swedes trust more? Culture, not welfare state policy. http://super-economy.blogspot.se/2010/10/why-do-swedes-trust-more-culture-not.html (accessed 2 October).

Sanandaji, T. (2012a) The American left's two Europes problem. *The American*, 29 February.

Sanandaji, T. (2012b) Poverty and causality. *Critical Review: A Journal of Politics and Society* 24(1): 51–59.

Sanandaji, T. and Sanandaji, N. (2014) Superentrepreneurs – and how your country can get them. London: Centre for Policy Studies.

Sanandaji, T. and Wallace, B. (2011) Fiscal illusion and fiscal obfuscation – tax perception in Sweden. *Independent Review* 16: 237–246.

Save the Children (2013) Surviving the First Day – State of the World's Mothers 2013.

Save the Children (2014) State of the World's Mothers 2014 – Saving Mothers and Children in Humanitarian Crises.

Schneider, F. and Williams, C. C. (2013) *The Shadow Economy*. London: Institute of Economic Affairs.

Skattebetalarnas Förening (2009) Lägre skatter – större jämlikhet.

Skogman Thoursie, P. (2004) Reporting sick: are sporting events contagious? *Journal of Applied Econometrics* 19: 809–823.

Spector, S. (2014) Den verkliga arbetslöshetens utveckling sedan 1996. Confederation of Swedish Enterprise.

Statistics Sweden (2012) Hur mycket jobbar vi i Sverige? Internationellt och över tid.

Statistics Sweden (2013a) Antal personer försörjda med sociala ersättningar och bidrag 2012, 15 August.

Statistics Sweden and Arbetslivsinstitutet (2002) Integration till svensk välfärd? Levnadsförhållanden Om invandrarnas välfärd på 90-talet, 96.

Statistics Sweden (2004) Inkomstfördelningsstudien 2004.

Statistics Sweden (2009). Arbetskraftsundersökningar (AKU), Sysselsättningen i Sverige 1963–2008.

Statistics Sweden (2013b) Ekonomiskt oberoende – långt väg kvar för EU:s kvinnor, Välfärd, 27 May.

Sundin, E. and Tillmar, M. (2008) Kvinnors företagande i spåren av offentlig sektors omvandling. In *Forskning om kvinnors företagande, presentation av projekten*. Stockholm: Vinnova.

Svenska Dagbladet (2011) Mikrofonskandalerna vi minns, 10 November.

Swedish Tax Agency (2007) Tax Statistical Yearbook of Sweden 2007.

Thakur, S., Keen, M., Horváth, B. and Cerra, V. (2003) *Sweden's Welfare State: Can the Bumblebee Keep Flying?* Washington, DC: International Monetary Fund.

Time Magazine (1976) Sweden: something souring in utopia, 19 July. Accessed through *Time Magazine*'s online archive at http://content.time.com/time/subscriber/article/0,33009, 914329-3,00.html on 31 January 2015.

Trabandt, M. and Uhlig, H. (2010) How far are we from the slippery slope? The Laffer curve revisited. European Central Bank Working Paper Series 1174.

Tyran, J.-R. and Sausgruber, R. (2005) Testing the Mill hypothesis of fiscal illusion. *Public Choice* 122(1/2): 39–68.

US Census Database. Census 2006–2008 American Community Survey 3-Year Estimates, Selected Population Profiles.

US Census 2000. Foreign born profiles.

Uslander, E. M. (2008) Where you stand depends upon where your grandparents sat – the inheritability of generalized trust. *Public Opinion Quarterly* 72: 725–740.

Wallen, F. and Fölster, S. (2009) Sjanghaja de som ligger. Hjalmarson & Högberg.

Washington Post (2011) Five economic lessons from Sweden, the rock star of the recovery, 24 June.

World Bank Database. Data over life span in different countries for 2011. Very small countries and special zones such as Hong Kong and the Virgin Islands have been removed from the comparison.

World Value Survey data for question V198 Justifiable: claiming government benefits.

Yosuf, K. (2010) Kronikk fra Kadra Yusuf: Til velferdsstaten skiller oss ad, article in Verdens Gang, 18 October.

ABOUT THE IEA

The Institute is a research and educational charity (No. CC 235 351), limited by guarantee. Its mission is to improve understanding of the fundamental institutions of a free society by analysing and expounding the role of markets in solving economic and social problems.

The IEA achieves its mission by:

- a high-quality publishing programme
- conferences, seminars, lectures and other events
- outreach to school and college students
- brokering media introductions and appearances

The IEA, which was established in 1955 by the late Sir Antony Fisher, is an educational charity, not a political organisation. It is independent of any political party or group and does not carry on activities intended to affect support for any political party or candidate in any election or referendum, or at any other time. It is financed by sales of publications, conference fees and voluntary donations.

In addition to its main series of publications the IEA also publishes a quarterly journal, *Economic Affairs*.

The IEA is aided in its work by a distinguished international Academic Advisory Council and an eminent panel of Honorary Fellows. Together with other academics, they review prospective IEA publications, their comments being passed on anonymously to authors. All IEA papers are therefore subject to the same rigorous independent refereeing process as used by leading academic journals.

IEA publications enjoy widespread classroom use and course adoptions in schools and universities. They are also sold throughout the world and often translated/reprinted.

Since 1974 the IEA has helped to create a worldwide network of 100 similar institutions in over 70 countries. They are all independent but share the IEA's mission.

Views expressed in the IEA's publications are those of the authors, not those of the Institute (which has no corporate view), its Managing Trustees, Academic Advisory Council members or senior staff.

Members of the Institute's Academic Advisory Council, Honorary Fellows, Trustees and Staff are listed on the following page.

The Institute gratefully acknowledges financial support for its publications programme and other work from a generous benefaction by the late Professor Ronald Coase.

Other papers recently published by the IEA include:

Fair Trade Without the Froth – A Dispassionate Economic Analysis of 'Fair Trade'
Sushil Mohan
Hobart Paper 170; ISBN 978-0-255-36645-8; £10.00

A New Understanding of Poverty – Poverty Measurement and Policy Implications
Kristian Niemietz
Research Monograph 65; ISBN 978-0-255-36638-0; £12.50

The Challenge of Immigration – A Radical Solution
Gary S. Becker
Occasional Paper 145; ISBN 978-0-255-36613-7; £7.50

Sharper Axes, Lower Taxes – Big Steps to a Smaller State
Edited by Philip Booth
Hobart Paperback 38; ISBN 978-0-255-36648-9; £12.50

Self-employment, Small Firms and Enterprise
Peter Urwin
Research Monograph 66; ISBN 978-0-255-36610-6; £12.50

Crises of Governments – The Ongoing Global Financial Crisis and Recession
Robert Barro
Occasional Paper 146; ISBN 978-0-255-36657-1; £7.50

… and the Pursuit of Happiness – Wellbeing and the Role of Government
Edited by Philip Booth
Readings 64; ISBN 978-0-255-36656-4; £12.50

Public Choice – A Primer
Eamonn Butler
Occasional Paper 147; ISBN 978-0-255-36650-2; £10.00

The Profit Motive in Education – Continuing the Revolution
Edited by James B. Stanfield
Readings 65; ISBN 978-0-255-36646-5; £12.50

Which Road Ahead – Government or Market?
Oliver Knipping & Richard Wellings
Hobart Paper 171; ISBN 978-0-255-36619-9; £10.00

The Future of the Commons – Beyond Market Failure and Government Regulation
Elinor Ostrom et al.
Occasional Paper 148; ISBN 978-0-255-36653-3; £10.00

Redefining the Poverty Debate – Why a War on Markets Is No Substitute for a War on Poverty
Kristian Niemietz
Research Monograph 67; ISBN 978-0-255-36652-6; £12.50

The Euro – the Beginning, the Middle … and the End?
Edited by Philip Booth
Hobart Paperback 39; ISBN 978-0-255-36680-9; £12.50

The Shadow Economy
Friedrich Schneider & Colin C. Williams
Hobart Paper 172; ISBN 978-0-255-36674-8; £12.50

Quack Policy – Abusing Science in the Cause of Paternalism
Jamie Whyte
Hobart Paper 173; ISBN 978-0-255-36673-1; £10.00

Foundations of a Free Society
Eamonn Butler
Occasional Paper 149; ISBN 978-0-255-36687-8; £12.50

The Government Debt Iceberg
Jagadeesh Gokhale
Research Monograph 68; ISBN 978-0-255-36666-3; £10.00

A U-Turn on the Road to Serfdom
Grover Norquist
Occasional Paper 150; ISBN 978-0-255-36686-1; £10.00

New Private Monies – A Bit-Part Player?
Kevin Dowd
Hobart Paper 174; ISBN 978-0-255-36694-6; £10.00

From Crisis to Confidence – Macroeconomics after the Crash
Roger Koppl
Hobart Paper 175; ISBN 978-0-255-36693-9; £12.50

Advertising in a Free Society
Ralph Harris and Arthur Seldon
With an introduction by Christopher Snowdon
Hobart Paper 176; ISBN 978-0-255-36696-0; £12.50

Selfishness, Greed and Capitalism: Debunking Myths about the Free Market
Christopher Snowdon
Hobart Paper 177; ISBN 978-0-255-36677-9; £12.50

Waging the War of Ideas
John Blundell
Occasional Paper 131; ISBN 978-0-255-36684-7; £12.50

Brexit: Directions for Britain Outside the EU
Ralph Buckle, Tim Hewish, John C. Hulsman, Iain Mansfield & Robert Oulds
Hobart Paperback 178; ISBN 978-0-255-36681-6; £12.50

Flaws and Ceilings – Price Controls and the Damage They Cause
Edited by Christopher Coyne and Rachel Coyne
Hobart Paperback 179; ISBN 978-0-255-36701-1; £12.50

Other IEA publications

Comprehensive information on other publications and the wider work of the IEA can be found at www.iea.org.uk. To order any publication please see below.

Personal customers

Orders from personal customers should be directed to the IEA:

Clare Rusbridge
IEA
2 Lord North Street
FREEPOST LON10168
London SW1P 3YZ
Tel: 020 7799 8907. Fax: 020 7799 2137
Email: sales@iea.org.uk

Trade customers

All orders from the book trade should be directed to the IEA's distributor:

NBN International (IEA Orders)
Orders Dept.
NBN International
10 Thornbury Road
Plymouth PL6 7PP
Tel: 01752 202301, Fax: 01752 202333
Email: orders@nbninternational.com

IEA subscriptions

The IEA also offers a subscription service to its publications. For a single annual payment (currently £42.00 in the UK), subscribers receive every monograph the IEA publishes. For more information please contact:

Clare Rusbridge
Subscriptions
IEA
2 Lord North Street
FREEPOST LON10168
London SW1P 3YZ
Tel: 020 7799 8907, Fax: 020 7799 2137
Email: crusbridge@iea.org.uk